BIG RIVER

BIG RIVER

THE ADVENTURES OF HUCKLEBERRY FINN

A MUSICAL PLAY

Book by William Hauptman
Adapted from the novel by Mark Twain

GROVE PRESS, INC./New York

This play is dedicated to Des, Roger, Rocco, Heidi, Bob, Ellen, Marjorie, Sarah, and to the memory of my father and Mark Twain.

WILLIAM HAUPTMAN

To my wife, Mary, and in memory of my Mom and Dad.

ROGER MILLER

Big River was originally presented at the American Repertory Theatre, Cambridge, Massachusetts, Robert Brustein, Artistic Director. It opened on February 22, 1984, with the following cast (in alphabetical order): Nina Bernstein, John Bottoms, Sandy Brown, Thomas Derrah, Mark Driscoll, Ben Evett, Jeremy Geidt, Ben Halley, Jr., Robert Joy, Jerome Kilty, Karen MacDonald, Harry S. Murphy, Marianne Owen, Tony Shaloub, and Alison Taylor. The production was directed by Des McAnuff, with sets by Heidi Landesman, costumes by Patricia McGourty, lighting by James F. Ingalls, sound by Randolph C. Head, orchestrations and musical direction by Michael S. Roth, production stage manager, John Grant-Philips.

Big River was subsequently presented at the LaJolla Playhouse, LaJolla, California, Des McAnuff, Artistic Director. It opened on June 24, 1984, with the following cast (in alphabetical order): Toby Alexander, John Anderson, William Bartram, Susan Berman, Melanie Chartoff, Ron Faber, Dann Florek, Brenda Foley, John Goodman, Ben Halley, Jr., Kyra Hider, Dee Hoty, Leah Maddrie, Paul McCrane, Tuck Milligan, Jack Murdock, Geoffrey Nauffts, and the Red Clay Ramblers. The production was directed by Des McAnuff, with sets by Heidi Landesman, costumes by Patricia McGourty, lights by Richard Riddell, sound by John Kilgore, choreography by Patrice Soriero, musical direction by Jack S. Herrick, music arranged by Jack S. Herrick and Christopher Frank. Production stage managers, Julie Haber and Marianne Cane.

Big River opened on Broadway at the Eugene O'Neill Theatre on April 25, 1985. It was presented by Rocco Landesman, Heidi Landesman, Rick Steiner, M. Anthony Fisher, and Dodger Productions. The *Big River* Company included (in alphabetical order): Rene Auberjonois, Evalyn Baron, Reathal Bean, Michael Brian, Susan Browning, Ralph Byers, Patti Cohenour, Gordon Connell, Carol Dennis, Aramis Estevez, John Goodman, Bob Gunton, Peggy Harmon, Andi Henig, Elmore James, Daniel Jenkins, Franz Jones, Ron Richardson, John Short, Jennifer Leigh Warren, and William Youmans. Onstage musicians: Don Brooks, John Guth, Kenny Kosek. The production was directed by Des McAnuff, with sets by Heidi Landesman, costumes by

Patricia McGourty, lighting by Richard Riddell, sound by Otts Munderloh, musical supervision by Danny Troob, orchestrations by Steven Margoshes and Danny Troob, dance and incidental music by John Richard Lewis, musical direction and vocal arrangements by Linda Twine, stage movement and fights by B. H. Barry, choreography by Janet Watson. Production stage manager, Frank Hartenstein.

The designer's intent was to keep the look and feel of 1840's stage craft. The backdrop is a sepia-toned etching of the Mississippi river, flowing toward us from the horizon. The river spills out of the backdrop, becoming a flight of wooden steps which descend to the stage floor. There, it flows as wooden planking on down to the apron. At the opening of the play, this is concealed by a scrim which looks like a gilded oval picture frame. Some elements are flown; some scenes are played on platforms, resembling piers, that track out of the wings. The raft, also tracked, can rotate and travel across the stage simultaneously.

CHARACTERS

(in order of appearance)

ACT ONE

In St. Petersburg, Missouri, and later on
the Illinois shore and Jackson's Island:

Mark Twain	Tom Sawyer	Townspeople
Huckleberry Finn	Ben Rogers	Slaves and Overseer
Jim	Joe Harper	Pap Finn
Widow Douglas	Simon	Judge Thatcher
Miss Watson	Dick	Strange Woman
	Schoolmaster	

On the river, south of St. Louis:
Slaves and Overseer on a flatboat

On the river, near Cairo, Illinois:
Two Men and a Slave on a skiff

On the river, somewhere in Kentucky:

The King	The Duke	Posse

ACT TWO

IN BRICKTOWN, ARKANSAS:

Hank	Andy	Tarts and Slaves
Lafe	Townspeople	of Bricktown

IN HILLSBORO, ARKANSAS:

Young Fool	Servant	Sheriff Bell
Mary Jane Wilkes	Counselor Robinson	Harvey Wilkes
Susan Wilkes	Alice	Man in Crowd
Joanna Wilkes,	Betsy	Mob
a hare-lip	Mourners	
	Furniture Movers	

ON A FARM NEAR HILLSBORO:

| Sally Phelps | Phelps Slaves | Patients |
| Silas Phelps | Doctor | Field Hands |

The action takes place along the
Mississippi River Valley, sometime in the late 1840's.

The roles are played by fourteen male and seven female actors,
and three onstage musicians.

MUSICAL NUMBERS

ACT ONE

Do Ya Wanna Go to Heaven?	The Company
The Boys	Tom and the Gang
Waitin' for the Light to Shine	Huck
Guv'ment	Pap
Hand for the Hog	Tom
I, Huckleberry, Me	Huck
Muddy Water	Jim and Huck
The Crossing	Slaves and Overseer
River in the Rain	Huck and Jim
When the Sun Goes Down in the South	Duke, King, Huck, Jim

MUSICAL NUMBERS

ACT TWO

The Royal Nonesuch	Duke and the Company
Worlds Apart	Jim and Huck
Arkansas	Young Fool
How Blest We Are	Betsy and Company
You Oughta Be Here with Me	Mary Jane, Susan, and Joanna
How Blest We Are (Reprise)	Company
Leavin's Not the Only Way to Go	Mary Jane, Jim, and Huck
Waitin' for the Light to Shine (Reprise)	Huck and Company
Free at Last	Jim and Company
River in the Rain (Reprise)	Huck and Jim
Muddy Water (Curtain call reprise)	Company

ACT ONE

Scene 1

Mark Twain *appears, smoking a cigar and standing before the frontispiece of* Huckleberry Finn, *which reads:*

> NOTICE:
> Persons attempting to find a motive
> in this narrative will be prosecuted;
> persons attempting to find a moral in
> it will be banished; persons attempting
> to find a plot in it will be shot.
>
> By order of the author
>
> MARK TWAIN

Huckleberry Finn *appears.*

Huck: You don't know about me, without you have read a book by the name of *The Adventures of Tom Sawyer,* but that ain't no matter. That book was written by Mr. Mark Twain, and he told the truth—mainly. There was some things he stretched, but mainly he told the truth. And I'm agoing to tell the truth, as I see it, in a story I'm enacting tonight.

*(***Jim*** appears, leaning against the proscenium with folded arms.)*

It's about me and my friend, a runaway slave named Jim, and a long journey we took together.

(The frontispiece flies out; **Jim** *and* **Twain** *exit. The* **Widow Douglas** *and her sister,* **Miss Watson,** *appear in their dining room.)*

Now the way the book winds up is this: Tom and me found the gold the robbers had hidden in Injun's Joe's Cave, and it made us rich.

Widow Douglas: Huckleberry!

Huck: My pap had disappeared . . .

Widow Douglas: Huckleberry!

Huck: So the Widow Douglas and her sister, Miss Watson, who owned Jim, took me for their son and allowed they would civilize me. *(He crosses into the dining room.)*

Widow Douglas: Huckleberry, where in the world have you been?

Huck: Staying after school to help the teacher.

Miss Watson: Not likely! He played hookey and went fishing, if I know a thing or two.

Widow Douglas: Is that true? Whatever am I going to do with you?

Miss Watson: Lock him in the closet and pray for his soul.

Widow Douglas: Maybe a whipping would do more good. I declare, if you don't do your lessons—

Miss Watson: And read your Bible—

Widow Douglas: You're going to end up as worthless as your father. *(Softening.)* But land sakes, you haven't even had your supper yet. Jim, give the boy a plate. A growing boy like you! You've got to put some flesh on those bones! Now you sit down here and eat your fill—but not until we've said the Blessing!

Huck *(to audience):* It got pretty rough living in that house, seeing they was so regular and decent in all their ways.

DO YA WANNA GO TO HEAVEN

Miss Watson:
>> Looka here, Huck, do you wanna go to heaven
>> Do you wanna go to heaven, well, I'll tell you
>>> right now
>> You better learn to read and you better learn your
>>> writin'
>> Or you'll never get to heaven 'cause you won't
>>> know how

Widow Douglas:
>> You may think that the whole thing is silly
>> But it isn't silly really

Miss Watson:
>> And I'll tell you right now
>> If you don't learn to read then you can't read your
>>> Bible

Widow Douglas:
>> And you'll never get to heaven 'cause you won't
>>> know how

Huck: Now Tom and me give our money to Judge Thatcher. He took and put it up at interest so it fetched us a dollar a day. That was mighty nice of him, but he thought that give him the right to tell me what sort of person I should be, too.

(Judge Thatcher *appears.)*

Judge Thatcher:
>> Looka here, Huck, now you better think it over
>> Do ya wanna be a loafer like your pappy is now
>> You better learn to read and you better learn your
>>> writin'

> Or you'll never get to heaven 'cause you won't
> know how

Huck: And Tom Sawyer wasn't above putting in his two cents worth either, saying I should be more like the fellows in those adventure books he was always reading.

(Tom Sawyer, *the* **Boys** *and a* **Schoolmaster** *appear.)*

Tom & Boys:
> Hey hey, ain't the situation
> Concernin' education aggravatin' and how
> Hey hey

Dick:
> Do you wanna get to heaven

Tom:
> Well you better get your lessons

Tom & Boys:
> Or you won't know how

Huck: In fact, sometimes it seemed like everybody in the whole blamed town of St. Petersburg was trying to tell me who I should be.

(Townspeople *appear.)*

Men:
> Huck Huck Huck Huck . . . (etc.)

Women:
> Looka here, Huck, do you wanna be a feller
> Like a feller really ought to be, I'll tell you right
> now
> You better learn to read and you better learn your
> writin'
> Or you'll never get to heaven 'cause you won't
> know how

Men:
> Hey hey, ain't the situation
> Concernin' education aggravatin' and how
> Hey hey, you want to go to heaven

All:
> Well you better get your lessons or you won't
> know how

(**Twain** *has reappeared; along with him,* **Slaves** *of St. Petersburg, who carry heavy bundles, and an* **Overseer** *with a whip.*)

Men *(chant):*
> Looka here, Huck, looka here, Huck
> Looka here
> Looka here, Huck, looka here

Boys:
> Read your Bible, Huck

Men:
> Looka here, Huck, looka here, Huck
> Looka here
> Looka here, Huck, looka here

Townswoman One:
> Do you wanna come to dinner

Men:
> Looka here, Huck, looka here, Huck
> Looka here
> Looka here, Huck, looka here . . . *(etc.)*

Women:	Boys:
Do you want to be a winner	
Do you want to think it over	Do your readin', Huck
Do you want to be a loafer	
Do you want to come to dinner	Do your writin', Huck
Do you want to be a winner	Get your lessons, Huck
Do you want to think it over	Read your Bible, Huck
Do you want to be a loafer	Read your Bible right now!

Dick:
> Do you wanna be a feller like you oughta be

Miss Watson:
> Do you want to go to heaven

(All actors close in on **Huck,** *who is still seated at the table.)*

All *(round):*
> You may think that the whole thing is silly
> But it isn't silly really and I'll tell you right now
> Tell you right now
> If you don't learn to read then you can't read your
>   Bible
> And you'll never get to heaven 'cause you won't
>   know how

> *(Unison.)*

> Hey hey, ain't the situation
> Concernin' education aggravatin' and how
> Hey hey, you wanna go to heaven
> Do you wanna go to heaven if you don't go to hell

> Do you wanna go to heaven
> Do you wanna go to heaven

> Well you better do your reading
> And you better read your Bible
> Do you wanna go to heaven if you don't go to hell

Miss Watson: Huck, you know how I've told you about the good place and the bad place?

Huck: Yes'm.

Miss Watson: If you don't change, you're going to the bad place.

Huck: I wish I was there.

Miss Watson: How can you say a wicked thing like that?

Huck: All I meant was, I want to go somewhere. I want a change; I'm not particular.

Miss Watson: Live like me, and you'll go to the good place.

Huck: Well, I can't see no advantage in going where you're going, so I've made up my mind I won't try for it.

Widow Douglas: That's it, you poor lost lamb! Stand up!

(She pulls him to his feet and spanks him with switch. **Huck** *looks at the audience and grins.)*

Huck: Then the widow'd give me a whipping, which cheered me up a little.

Widow Douglas: Now you go upstairs—

Miss Watson: Say your prayers—

Widow Douglas: And go to sleep!

*(***Huck*** *crosses away from them as all actors clear the stage and darkness falls.)*

Scene 2

Huck *(to audience):* But that night, instead of sleeping, I shinnied down the drainpipe and got clean away. It was a lonesome night. There was only a few lights burning in the whole town of St. Petersburg, where there was sick folks, maybe. And the wind was trying to whisper something to me, like a ghost that can't make itself understood, so it's got to go about every night, grieving. *(A hooting sound.* **Huck** *grins and hoots in reply.)* Tom Sawyer! Is that you?

(Tom Sawyer *appears.)*

Tom: Come along, Huck!

Huck: Where we going?

Tom: Injun Joe's Cave!

Huck *(to audience):* So I followed him, through the graveyard and down to the river. Then we took the tow-path until we come to the big scar on the hillside and there we crawled through a hole and into the cave, whose walls was all of clay—damp, sweaty, and cold as a corpse.

(Tom *lights a candle as they enter the cave.* **Ben Rogers, Jo Harper, Dick,** *and* **Simon** *are already there.)*

Tom *(producing a paper):* Now we're going to start this gang of robbers and call it Tom Sawyer's Gang.

Ben Rogers: What's the line of business of this gang?

Tom: Nothing, only robbery and murder.

Ben: Bully.

Tom: Whoever wants to join has got to take this oath, and sign his name in blood.

Jo: What's it say, Tom?

Tom: It swears every boy to stick to the gang, and never tell any of its secrets. And if he does, he must have his throat cut, then have his carcass burnt up and the ashes scattered around, and his name blotted off the list, and never mentioned by the gang but have a curse put on it and be forgot forever.

Ben: Real beautiful, Tom!

Simon: You get that out of your own head?

Tom *(modestly):* Some. The rest is out of pirate and robber books.

Ben: Be a good idea to kill the families of the boys who tell the secrets too.

Tom: I'll write it in.

Jo: But here's Huck Finn—he ain't got a family.

Dick: Then we got to rule him out.

Ben: Yeah, every boy's got to have a family or somebody to kill, or it wouldn't be fair and square for the others.

Huck *(to audience):* I almost cried when I thought they weren't going to allow me in Tom Sawyer's gang, but just then I got an idea. *(To* **Boys:**) There's Miss Watson, the lady who's taking care of me—you can kill her.

Ben: Bully.

Tom: There you go; she'll do. Huck can come in. Now—everybody stick their finger with this knife to get some blood, and we'll seal the oath.

(They prick their fingers and pass the oath around, having a grand time. As they do they sing.)

THE BOYS

Tom:
> Well if the bunch of us all stick together
> And we all go down as one
> We could be highway robbers
> We could be killers just out to have fun
> And if any of you can't keep a secret
> We'll cut your throat if you tell
> Then lay you down 'neath six feet of ground
> 'Cause we were born to raise hell

> All together now

Boys:
> We are the boys

Tom:
> All together

Boys:
> Forever and always

Tom:
> All together now

Boys:
> We are the boys
> We're together forever and always

Ben: Who we going to rob? Houses? Or cattle? Or people?

Tom: That ain't no sort of style! We are highwaymen. We stop stages and kill the people and steal their watches and money.

Huck:
> Well if the bunch of us all, now listen,
> 'Cause here's the part I like the best
> If we all got a hold of some horses
> We could ride like the boys out West

Ben:
We could hoot, shoot, and we could holler

Dick:
We could ride like the devil wind

Simon:
Then go back to the cave and sleep all day

Boys:
And do it the next night again

Tom & Dick:
All together now

Boys:
We are the boys

Tom & Dick:
All together

Boys:
Forever and always

Tom & Dick:
All together now

Boys:
We are the boys
We're together forever and always

Simon: Do we always kill the people?

Tom: Oh, certainly. It's best. Some authorities think different, but mostly it's considered best just to kill them.

Jo: Do we kill the women too?

Tom: Jo Harper, if I was as ignorant as you, I wouldn't let on! Kill the women? No—you fetch 'em to the cave, and you're always as polite as pie to 'em; and by and by, they fall in love with you and never want to go home anymore.

Jo: Well, if that's the way, then I'm agreed.

Tom: Good.

Boys:
>Well if the bunch of us all stick together
>>well if the bunch of us all (stick together)
>
>And we all go down as one
>>and we all go down (as one)
>
>We could be highway robbers
>>we could be highway robbers
>
>We could be killers just out to have fun

Tom:
>And if the bunch of us all form a circle
>And surround all the ladies of the town

Tom & Huck:
>I say hey hey hey we'll take them to the cave
>And dance them till they all fall down

Boys:
>All together now
>We are the boys
>All together
>Forever and always
>All together now
>We are the boys
>We're together forever and always
>We are the boys
>All together
>Forever and always
>All together now
>We are the boys
>We're together forever and always

Tom: Everybody signed?

Jo *(trying to prick his finger with knife):* Ouch.

Ben: You big crybaby.

Jo: Am not.

Ben: Are so.

Jo: Am not.

Ben: Are so.

Jo: You call me a crybaby, I'm going to tell everybody the secrets!

Tom: Hold on! No fighting amongst club members. *(Gives* **Jo** *a nickel.)*

Jo: But . . .

Tom: Here's a nickel; now keep your trap shut.

Simon: Tom, I got to be going home anyway.

Tom: All right, go home—then we'll get together next week and rob some people and kill some people.

Ben: I can only get out on Sundays. Let's begin on Sunday.

Jo: It'd be wicked to do it on Sunday.

Ben: Great big sissy.

Jo: Am not!

Ben: Are so!

Tom *(averting an argument):* Let's just agree to get together and fix a date soon as possible.

Ben: So long, Tom, Huck.

(The **Boys** *blow out their candles and go.* **Tom** *and* **Huck** *come downstage and sit on apron.)*

Tom: They don't seem to know nothing, somehow, do they?—perfect sapheads.

Huck: How's your life with Aunt Polly?

Tom: Dismal. How's yours with the widow?

Huck *(lighting his pipe):* She won't let me smoke my pipe.

Tom *(producing his own pipe):* Aunt Polly won't let me either.

Huck: Ain't that just the way with people, to get down on something they don't know nothing about? But it's not the widow, it's Miss Watson who's so blamed tiresome. She says all a body has to do in the good place is go around all day with a harp and sing. So I asked her if Tom Sawyer would be there.

Tom: What'd she say?

Huck: Not by a considerable sight. *(They laugh.)* I was glad about that, 'cause I want you and me to be together. What we going to do with all our money, Tom?

Tom: I don't know, Huck. Just think of it: six thousand dollars apiece—all gold—found right here in this cave. . . . What *are* we going to do with it?

Huck: Light out for the western territories.

Tom: Thunderation!

Huck: That's what I been thinking.

Tom: It's a capital idea! I'll go with you!

Huck: Will you?

Tom: Just as soon as this year of school is out.

Huck: You don't mean it, do you, Tom?

Tom: Sure I do, just wait and see. Come spring, you and me'll steal some horses and go live amongst the Injuns. Say, it's getting late, we'd better be going. *(Rises, socks Huck on arm.)* See you in class.

(Tom *exits.)*

Huck *(to audience):* But I knowed Tom Sawyer didn't mean it, no more than he meant all that talk about robbing and killing. And if he wouldn't go with me, who would?

WAITIN' FOR THE LIGHT TO SHINE

I have lived in the darkness for so long
I am waitin' for the light to shine

Far beyond horizons I have seen
Beyond the things I've been
Beyond the dreams I've dreamed
Are the things I've done
In fact each and every one
Are the way that I was taught to run

I am waitin' for the light to shine
I am waitin' for the light to shine
I have lived in the darkness for so long
I'm waitin' for the light to shine

Scene 3

Huck *enters the house and goes to his bedroom.*

Huck: When I got back to the widow's, I went up to my bedroom, thinking I'd rather live in a sugar hogshead again, like in the old days and be free and satisfied. I had a strange feeling that trouble was coming, but I wasn't sure yet when it was going to fall on me, or what it was going to be . . .

(Huck's *father rises up from behind the bed. His face is tree-toad white; his eyes shine through tangled, greasy hair that covers his forehead like vines.)*

Pap: Starchy clothes . . .

Huck *(gives an involuntary yell):* There sat Pap, his old self.

Pap *(fingering his shirt):* You think you're a good deal of a big bug, don't you?

Huck: Maybe I am, and maybe I ain't.

Pap *(laughing unpleasantly):* You got a bed . . . a look-ing-glass . . . why, there ain't no end to your airs. You're educated, so they say. You can read and write.

Huck: I do.

Pap: Think you're better than your father now? Your mother couldn't read before she died, couldn't write nuther. None of your family could, before they died. I can't. *(Giving him a book.)* Say—let me hear you read.

Huck *(reading):* George Washington was the first President of the United States . . .

Pap: It's so. You can do it. I had my doubts when they told me. *(Exploding, he slaps the book away.)* You drop that school, you hear me! I'll lay for you, my smarty, and if I catch you around that school, I'll tan you good! *(Quietly.)* They say you're rich—how's that?

Huck: They lie, that's how!

Pap *(exploding again):* I been in town three days, and I ain't heard nothing but about you being rich! You give me that money—I want it!

(Widow Douglas *and* **Miss Watson** *enter.)*

Widow Douglas: What's all this commotion about! Old Finn—what are you doing here!

Pap *(politely, taking off his battered hat):* Hello, Widow Douglas, Miss Watson. I just come to see my boy—you know I love him so.

Widow Douglas: If you love him so, where have you been for the past year?

Pap: Upriver and down, looking for some place where they don't hold a man's past against him. Then I heard about my son's good fortune. By the way—where is the money?

Huck: I ain't got it!

Miss Watson: Huck—Honor Thy Father.

Huck: I give it to Judge Thatcher.

Pap: Judge Thatcher! We'll see about that!

(**Judge Thatcher** *appears, sober and dignified.*)

Huck *(to audience):* First thing in the morning we went to see Judge Thatcher.

Judge Thatcher: Huck has made a nominal transfer of the money to me, and I've put it in trust. Meanwhile, I pay him the interest—three hundred dollars a year.

Pap *(seeing a way out):* Three hundred dollars a year. . . . *(Politely.)* Well now, Your Honor, these women have done a fine job of bringing my boy up, anyone could see that. But courts mustn't separate families, and now that I'm back I want him to live with me.

Widow Douglas: All he wants is the interest!

Pap: You do me wrong! Your Honor, I'm a man who's been often misunderstood—

Judge Thatcher: I can believe that.

Pap: But up river I met a man who showed me I'd been a fool and fooled away my life! Here's a hand that was the hand of a hog, but it ain't no more. It's a clean hand now, so take hold of it, shake it, and don't be afeard, because I tell you, I'm a new man!

Miss Watson: If it's so, this is the holiest day on record.

Widow Douglas: Huck—who do you want to live with?

Huck: I still like the old ways . . . but I'm getting to like the new ones, too, a little.

Pap *(dropping pretense):* He's mine! And so's that money! I'm gonna get a lawyer to take you to trial, Judge Thatcher. Meanwhile, the boy stays with me!

Widow Douglas: You can't take Huck!

Judge Thatcher: No, there's nothing we can do about that. Legally, you're still the boy's father. But if you harm him in any way . . . there will be consequences. *(To* **Huck:***)* I'm sorry, son. I never thought your father would come back. *(To* **Pap:***)* Things would have been simpler if you'd stayed dead.

(Judge Thatcher, Widow Douglas, *and* **Miss Watson** *exit.)*

Pap: First thing I'm going to do is get you away from that school. I got a cabin over on the Illinois shore—They can't touch us over there, and we can live real good on three hundred dollars a year!

Scene 4

Effortlessly, **Pap** *drags* **Huck** *across the stage and throws him to the floor of a cabin in the woods.*

Huck *(to audience):* And that's just what my pap done. Took me to his old log hut in a place where it was so woody you couldn't find it if you didn't know where it was.

Pap *(throwing fish at* **Huck***):* Clean those fish. *(He sits on a stool and drinks from a jug, well pleased with himself.)* That Judge—ain't I going to show him who's Huck Finn's boss? And they call this a government! What sort of government is it that'll try to take a man's son away from him, huh?

Huck: Well . . .

Pap: A man's son, which he's had all the trouble and anxiety of raising.

Huck *(cleaning fish):* I don't know, Pap.

Pap: Sometimes I've a mighty notion to leave the country for good and all; yes, and I'll tell Judge Thatcher so to his face!

GUV'MENT

Well . . . you dad gum guv'ment
You sorry so and so's
You got your damn hands
In every pocket of my clothes

Well, you dad gum, dad gum, dad gum guv'ment
Oh, don't you know
Oh, don't you love 'em sometimes

You dad gum guv'ment
You better pay attention
You're sittin' up there like a fool's convention

Well, you dad gum, dad gum, dad gum guv'ment
Oh, don't you know
Oh, don't you love 'em sometimes

Well, you soul sellin' no good sons-of-a
Dead pan shoe fittin' fire starters
I ought to tear your

No good God dang pre ambulatory bone frame
And nail it to your guv'ment walls
All of you
You bastards.

You dad gum guv'ment
You sorry rakafratchits
You got yourself an itch and you want me to
    scratch it

(Drinks from jug.)

Well, you dad gum, you dad gum
You dad gum

You dad gum guv'ment
You sorry sons-of-bitches
You got your damn hands in every pocket of my
    britches
Well, you dad gum, dad gum, dad gum guv'ment
Oh don't you know
Don't you love 'em sometimes

Huck: Light the stove, Pap, and I'll roll these fish in corn-meal.

Pap: Don't you like livin' out here in the woods with your old pap? We'll go fishing and hunting. You can take up cussing again if you like—I ain't got no objections. You can get up when you please, and you don't have to eat off no plate.

Huck: It could be right jolly—if you didn't drink so.

Pap *(softly):* . . . Do me a favor son. *(When* **Huck** *won't look at him.)* Would you do me a favor?

Huck: What?

Pap: Remember your old father from a better day.

Huck *(moved):* Don't talk that way, Pap. We've had some pretty good times, take it all around.

Pap *(drinking from his jug and brooding):* Just when a man's got his son all raised up at last, ready to go to work and do something for him to give him a rest—they try to take him away. What kind of government is that? *(Picking up a hickory stick and lurching into* **Huck's** *path.)* Will you stand still when I'm talking to you?

(Huck *shoves him down, breaks the stick and throws it to the floor.)*

So that's how they teach you to act. There ain't no end to your airs, is there?

Huck *(taking his shoulder):* Come on, Pap. I'll help you to your cot.

(As they stagger toward the cot, **Pap** *suddenly screams hoarsely and points to the floor.)*

Pap: What's that?

Huck: A broken stick.

Pap: It's a cottonmouth. Don't go near it.

Huck: It's just a broken stick, Pap.

Pap: I'm snakebit. Cottonmouth bit me.

Huck *(trying to get him onto cot):* No, Pap. You been bit by that forty-rod whiskey, that's all.

Pap: There's another. Get him off!

Huck *(holding him down):* You're sick, Pap! You got the delirium tremens. Now lie still with the blanket over you and I'll get you a drink of water. Will you lie still?

Pap: You've gotten so big and strong. I remember when you was just a tadpole.

Huck *(bringing him a dipper of water):* Sleep, Pap. (**Pap** *closes his eyes, and* **Huck** *speaks to audience.)* That's when I first thought about running off. But I couldn't leave Pap this way. I went to the window to see if daylight was coming.

*(***Pap*** *rises silently, opens his Barlow-Knife, moves toward* **Huck.**)

Won't this night never end?

Pap: Angel of Death! I'll kill you, then you won't come for me no more!

(Roaring, he chases **Huck** *around the cabin. As he raises his knife to strike,* **Huck** *hits him under the chin with a stool.* **Pap** *staggers, falls back onto his cot.)*

Tired . . . I'll rest a minute, then kill you. *(Slips his knife under himself and falls asleep.)*

Scene 5

Huck *(to audience):* Then I just wanted to get away from my pap, and the money, and all the trouble it caused me. Next day, Pap went to town.

(Pap *rises, glares at* **Huck,** *and exits.)*

I done something so bloody I shouldn't tell you about it— but I will. I caught a wild pig and chopped down the door of the cabin. Then I cut the pig's throat and spilled blood all over everything. So they'd think somebody broke in and murdered me. Oh, I throwed in all the fancy touches. Tom Sawyer couldn't a done it better! And as Tom always said—a man's best friend is a hog.

(Tom *appears and, as* **Huck** *does all this, sings.)*

HAND FOR THE HOG
Tom:
> Well, I always heard but I ain't too sure
> That a man's best friend is a mangy cur
> But I kinda favor the hog myself
> How about a hand for the hog

Ya say a hog ain't nothin' but a porky thing
Little forked feet with a nosey ring
Pickle them feet, folks
How about a hand for the hog

If you took a notion I bet
A good hog would make a hell of a pet
You could teach him to ride and hunt
You could clean him up and let him sit up front

Huck: Then I got some matches, some fishhooks, a spyglass and some coffee, and crossed over to Jackson's Island in Pap's canoe.

(As **Huck** *paddles,* **Tom** *concludes the song.)*

Tom:
In the scheme of things and the way things go
You might get bit by the old Fido
But not by the gentle porker friend
How about a hand for the hog

A feller and a hog had a comedy act
The feller was terrible as a matter of fact
That hog was a funny sucker though
How about a hand for the hog

If you took a notion I'll bet
You could teach a hog to smoke a cigarette
Well it might take a little bit of time
But hell, what's time to a hog?

Well, the way I see it,
It looks like this
Either you ain't or either you is
A true blue lover of the swine, folks
How about a hand for the hog
Thank you.

(Tom *disappears.* **Huck** *stares up at a yellowish crescent moon.)*

Huck: The sky looks ever so deep when you look up in the moonlight. Everything was dead quiet, and it looked late, and *smelt* late—you know what I mean. Just me and the drift logs and the moon.

(He drags the canoe ashore on Jackson's Island.)

When I got to Jackson's Island, I was tired and sort of lonesome. There ain't no better way to put in time when you are lonesome than sleep. You can't stay so; you soon get over it. So I slept for the better part of three days.

(When the sun rises, **Huck** *lies in a cool green glade, filled with the sound of singing birds.)*

I was woke up by this deep boom.

(Thump of a cannon going off. **Huck** *looks through his spyglass. Through a scrim upstage, we see the people on board the ferry.)*

Through my spyglass I seen the ferryboat crossing the river. They were firing off a cannon to make my body rise to the top, and floating loaves of bread loaded with quick-silver—'cause that's supposed to go right to a drowned carcass and stop. Then I knowed my plan had worked and they thought I was dead. There's Pap . . . and Judge Thatcher . . . and the widow and Miss Watson . . . and Ben Rogers and Jo Harper, and there's Tom Sawyer! *(Laughs.)* The look on their faces!

Widow Douglas: Huckleberry! Huckleberry!

(The ferryboat is gone.)

Huck: But when they were gone, I felt almost lonely again. So I started exploring the island. I was the boss of it; it all belonged to me, so to say. And I was thinking: here

was a place where a body didn't have to be nobody but
himself.

I, HUCKLEBERRY, ME

I, Huckleberry, me
Somewhere sittin' underneath some tree
Somewhere maybe fishin'
Maybe someplace sittin' just wishin' I was fishin'

Oh, I, Huckleberry, me
Hereby declare myself to be
Nothing ever other than
Exactly what I am

And I'll never change for no one
No matter what they say
If I want to smoke in church I'll smoke
If I want to pray I'll pray, oh

I, Huckleberry, me
Hereby declare myself to be
Nothing ever other than
Exactly what I am

(**Huck** *discovers a dead skunk.*)

Dead skunk—right good for curing warts! *(He throws
skunk away.)*

And I'll never change for no one
No matter what they say
If I want to go to school, I'll go
If I want to stay away, I'll stay, oh

I, Huckleberry, me
Hereby declare myself to be
Nothing ever other than
Exactly what I am

> Nothing ever other than
> Exactly what I am

(As he finishes the song, **Huck** *comes face to face with* **Jim.** *Both recoil.)*

Hello, Jim!

Jim: Get back in the river where you belong, and don't do nothing to ole Jim, who was always your friend!

Huck: Jim, I'm not dead! I'm alive—and ever so glad to see you!

Jim: You ain't a ghost, is you?

Huck: Touch me—I'm solid enough. I had to run away from Pap. He got the delirium tremens and tried to stab me with his Barlow-Knife. So I faked the whole thing.

*(***Jim** *just keeps staring.* **Huck** *addresses the audience.)*

I talked along, but Jim just stood there. Finally he says—

Jim: See those birds flyin' low? That means rain. Let's go to my camp.

Huck: I followed Jim to a lean-to he'd built on the Illinois side.

(A flash of lightning and a roll of thunder. They cross to a lean-to. An enormous catfish hangs from a line. There is a trunk, and a raft of logs nearby.)

You got a great place here, Jim! That must be the biggest catfish ever pulled out of the Mississippi River!

Jim *(taking out knife and cutting down the fish):* Found him on my trotline this morning. I was just getting ready to clean him up.

Huck: I never seen a bigger one . . . what's all this?

Jim: Trash come floating down on the high water.

Huck *(opening the trunk):* Here's a calico gown . . . and some seegars . . . there must be a flood somewheres upriver . . . and look at this raft!

Jim: That came floating down too.

Huck: Jim? What *are* you doing here?

Jim: You wouldn't tell on me if I was to tell you?

Huck: Blamed if I would, Jim.

Jim: Huck—I run off.

Huck: Jim!

Jim: You said you wouldn't tell.

Huck: And I'll stick to it, Jim, honest Injun. People can call me a dirty abolitionist and despise me for it—that don't make no difference. I ain't a-going to tell and I ain't a-going back there anyways—so let's hear about it.

Jim: Miss Watson always say she won't sell me. But I notice lately there's been a slave trader around the place considerable. The night you was killed, I creep to the door, and I hear the missus telling the Widow Douglas she's going to sell me down to New Orleans. She don't want to, but she can get eight hundred dollars for me, and it's such a big stack of money, she can't refuse. I never hear the rest. I light out. *(He cuts open the belly of the catfish—bloodlessly—and several objects spill out.)* Big fish like this eat all sorts of trash in his years.

Huck: I'll say. Here's a spool.

Jim: And a horseshoe.

Huck (*picks up a hard little sphere*): What's this?

Jim: Must a been in there a long time to coat it over so. (**Jim** *cuts open the sphere and hands* **Huck** *a coin.*)

Huck: It's gold.

Jim: What sort of writing is that on it?

Huck: Spanish . . . I think. This is a Spanish d'bloon, Jim, it's pirate gold! Why I reckon this fish could be a hundred years old. Do you reckon so, Jim?

Jim (*nodding*): He go along on the bottom. Eat the little ones. Get older and older and bigger and bigger. He here before people come maybe. Before this was a country. When there was nothing here but that big river . . . (*He grabs* **Huck's** *arm.*) I'm going down that river, Huck. To Cairo, where the Mississippi joins the Ohio. Then I'm following the Ohio north, to the Free States. I'm going down on that raft, and I'm getting my freedom!

Huck: I'm going with you, Jim!

Jim: You get in a powerful lot of trouble, helping Jim. You might find yourself hangin' from a cottonwood tree.

Huck: You can't do it alone. But if I come along, I can tell people you belong to me, and they won't bother you.

Jim (*greatly moved*): You'd do that for Jim? Then you a friend, Huck.

Scene 6

Huck *(looking up):* Storm's clearing. Jim, you provision the raft. I'll slip over to the Missouri shore.

Jim: But it's dangerous, Huck. What you want to do that for?

Huck: Why, just to see what's going on.

Jim *(pulling a calico gown out of the trunk):* Here's a notion: Couldn't you put this on and go as a girl?

Huck: That's a blamed good notion, Jim. *(Struggling into it.)* This way nobody'll know me.

Jim: You better hope nobody sees you. You got to go by dark and be careful.

Huck: Don't worry.

Jim: This ain't no time to go playing the fool. Jim won't rest until you come back. He's depending on you!

*(While **Jim** loads the raft, **Huck** crosses to a cabin on the Missouri shore. Inside, a **Strange Woman** sits sewing by a wood stove.)*

Huck *(to audience):* Well, of course I shouldn't have gone, but I was dying to find out what people were saying about me, now that I was murdered. When I got to the Missouri shore, there was a light in the window of a shanty. Peeping through, I seen there was only a woman there, so I knocked on the door and made up my mind I wouldn't forget I was a girl. *(Knocks.)*

Strange woman *(answering door):* Who might you be?

Huck *(little girl's voice):* Sarah Williams.

Strange Woman: What are you doing out so late, child?

Huck: Looking for my uncle, Abner Williams. I'm not from these parts. Do you know him?

Strange Woman: No—but go in and rest a spell.

Huck *(curtseys):* Thank you, ma'am. *(He sits in a chair across from hers.)*

Strange Woman: My husband'll be home in half an hour. He can help you find this Abner Williams. Don't you want to take off your bonnet?

Huck: No. I guess you've heard about the murder of this boy, Huck Finn?

Strange Woman: 'Deed I have.

Huck: Who do you think done it?

Strange Woman: At first, some said his father. Thread this needle for me—what did you say your name was, honey?

Huck: Mary Williams.

Strange Woman: I thought you said it was Sarah when you first come in.

Huck *(struggling to thread the needle):* Oh, yes, ma'am, I did. Sarah Mary Williams; that's the way of it. So people think his father done it?

Strange Woman: Come on now, what's your real name? Bill? Or Tom? Or Bob?

Huck: Please don't poke fun at a poor girl like me, ma'am.

Strange Woman: I know your secret!

Huck: Well . . .

Strange Woman: You're a runaway apprentice, aren't you?

Huck: All right. My name's George Peters and my parents are dead. The law bonded me to this mean old farmer out in the country—

Strange Woman: Well try to remember it, George. Don't forget and go telling me it's Alexander. Bless you, child, I won't tell on you. You're safe with me. Just be thankful you're not that runaway nigger Jim, the one folks are saying murdered Huck Finn.

Huck: *Jim!*

Strange Woman: So they think, and we'll soon find out. This morning, I seen some smoke over yonder on what they call Jackson's Island, where nobody ever goes; and I says to myself, like as not that slave's hiding over there. There's a big reward, and my husband and another man went to get a gun and borrow a boat. They'll be going over there at midnight.

Huck: I got to go myself, ma'am. There's folks in Goshen who'll take care of me.

Strange Woman: Go then. You ain't any sort of girl, but I reckon you might fool men. Only when you thread a needle, hold the needle still and poke the thread at it—that's what a girl does. *(Shouting after him as he leaves.)* And don't forget your name, Sarah Mary Williams George Alexander Peters!

(Huck *crosses back to Jackson's Island, throwing off the dress as he goes.)*

Huck: I got back in the canoe and shoved back to the island in a hurry. Jim was laid out sound asleep when I got there. *(Pulling* **Jim** *to his feet.)* Get up and hump yourself, Jim! They're after us, and we ain't got a minute to lose.

Jim: I didn't get all the provisions aboard.

Huck: Forget that! Just shove her out and I'll lay into that pole, Jim.

(They sing as they pole the raft out into the current. The scrim behind them goes transparent, revealing the river; then flies out, just before the song ends.)

MUDDY WATER

Jim:
Look out for me, oh muddy water
Your mysteries are deep and wide
And I got a need for going someplace
And I got a need to climb upon your back and
ride
You can look for me
When you see me comin'
I may be runnin' I don't know
I may be tired and runnin' fever
But I'll be headed south to the mouth of the Ohio

Huck & Jim:
Look out for me, oh muddy water
Your mysteries are deep and wide
And I got a need for goin' someplace

And I got a need to climb upon your back and
  ride

Jim:

Well, I been down to the pain and sorrow
Of no tomorrows comin' in
But I put my pole to the river bottom
And I've got to hide some place to find myself
  again

Huck & Jim:

Look out for me, oh muddy water
Your mysteries are deep and wide
And I got a need for goin' someplace
And I got a need to climb upon your back and
  ride

Look out for me, oh muddy water
Your mysteries are deep and wide
And I got a need for goin' someplace
And I got a need to climb upon your back and
  ride

Look out for me, oh muddy water
Your mysteries are deep and wide
And I got a need for goin' someplace
And I got a need to climb upon your back and
  ride

Scene 7

Huck *and* **Jim,** *floating on the raft in the moonlight.*

Huck: We'll travel by night. Eight nights should fetch us down to Cairo, where the Mississippi joins the Ohio. Then we'll sell this raft, maybe, and catch a steamboat north, to the Free States. Think we're going to make it?

Jim: Give me your left hand.

Huck: You know all the signs, do you, Jim?

Jim: I know most every one there is.

Huck: What do you see?

Jim *(examining his hand):* Considerable trouble and considerable joy.

Huck: That ain't much help. But we're a-going to make it, Jim—we got luck.

Jim: So long as we don't do nothing foolish.

Huck: You mean like looking at the new moon over your left shoulder?

Jim: That, or touching a snakeskin with your bare hands.

Huck: Looking at the new moon's the worst. Ole Hank Bunker did it, and bragged about it. And not two years later he got drunk and fell off the water tower, and spread himself out so he was just a kind of layer, as you may say, and they had to slide him between two doors for a coffin.

Jim: Look sharp. There's something up ahead.

Huck *(to audience):* The river was still in flood, and all sorts of things had come floating down on it.

(They drift past ghostly sights, half seen in the almost total darkness.)

Look. There's a house, Jim, all tilted over like. And a steamboat killed herself on a rock.

Jim: And a dead body.

(A corpse floats in the river alongside the raft. **Jim** *looks at it closely.)*

He's drowned. . . . I reckon he's only been dead a few hours.

Huck *(eagerly):* I never saw a dead body before!

Jim *(with strange intensity):* No, Huck! Don't look at his face—it's too ghastly! Let him go on his way. *(He releases the corpse. The river carries it out of sight.)*

Huck: What's wrong with you, Jim?

Jim: Don't talk no more 'bout it.

Huck: Why wouldn't you let me look at him?

Jim: You want him to come back and haunt us? A man who's not buried is more likely to go a-haunting than one who's planted and comfortable.

Huck *(to audience):* That sounded pretty reasonable, so I didn't say no more.

Jim: Here's daylight.

Huck: *(to audience):* When the sun rose, we tied up the raft where nobody could see it and slept; and later I told Jim stories about the great kings of the world.

*(**Huck** and **Jim** are lying on the raft in the green shade of the river bank. Pencils of sunlight fall through the leaves. The cicadas drone.)*

Jim: I never knowed there was so many kings. Onliest one I ever heard of was King Solomon—'less you count the kings on a deck of cards. Ain't no kings in America, is there, Huck?

Huck: Some say King Louis the Fourteen of France had a little boy, the Dolphin, who came over here to America when his pa got his head chopped off.

Jim: But if there ain't no kings here, he'd be lonely. What would he do? He couldn't get no situation.

Huck: Join the police force, maybe. Or teach people how to speak French.

Jim: Why don't the French people speak the way we do?

Huck: Jim, you couldn't understand a word of it. *(Sitting up.)* Suppose someone was to come up to you and say *polly voo franzy,* what would you think?

Jim: I wouldn't think nothing; I'd take an' bust him in the head—that is, if he weren't white.

Huck: It ain't calling you anything. It's just saying do you know how to speak French?

Jim: Well then, why don't he just *say* it?

Huck: He *is* saying it; that's the French way of saying it.

Jim: Well, it's a blame ridiculous way of saying it, and I don't want to hear no more about it.

Huck: I give up, Jim; it's impossible to learn you anything.

Jim: How much do a king get, Huck?

Huck: As much as he wants; everything belongs to him. Why, he could get—a thousand dollars a day.

Jim: Ain't *that* gay? And what he got to do to get it?

Huck: Nothing.

Jim: Nothing?

Huck: Nothing.

Jim: You mean he just lays around, like we're doing?

Huck: 'Cept when things is dull. Then he fusses with the Parliament. And if everybody doesn't go just so, he chops their heads off.

Jim *(rising):* Then I reckon we're just as well off as kings.

Huck: 'Cept we ain't rich.

Jim: Well, I got more money now than I ever had. I owns myself—and I'm worth eight hundred dollars. Come on, let's fix something to eat.

Huck *(to audience):* Then we'd have catfish and cornbread, or sometimes, I lifted a chicken from a farmer and took her along. Pap always said, take a chicken when you get the chance, because if you don't want it, you can easy find somebody that does, and a good deed ain't never forgot. I never seen Pap when he didn't want the chicken himself, but that's what he used to say anyway. When it got dark, we'd shove off.

(Now they are on the river again. The moon is waning, and sheds less light.)

Jim: Light that lantern, Huck. We don't want to get run down.

(Huck lights the lantern hanging from a stick on the bow. His face can be seen in its orange glow.)

Huck: Sometimes I'd catch myself thinking about that dead man.

Jim: Forget it, Huck. It'll bring bad luck.

Huck: But I couldn't keep from studying over it, wondering who he was.

Jim: Look yonder!

(Spread across the horizon are the lights of St. Louis.)

Huck: The fifth night, we floated past St. Louis.

Jim: What a wonderful spread of lights.

Huck: They say there's twenty or thirty thousand people living in St. Louis, but I never believed it till now.

Jim: Lord, it looks like the whole world lit up.

Huck: And not a sound: everybody must be asleep.

Jim: Three more nights should fetch us to Cairo!

(Singing is heard in the distance.)

Huck: Listen! What's that?

(A flatboat appears, rowed along by a crew of Slaves in chains who sing as they row. In the stern is a White Overseer with a shotgun.)

Jim: Slaves who tried to run off, like me. But they got caught. Now they crossing back.

Huck: How do you figure that?

Jim: I hears it in their singing.

THE CROSSING

Slaves:
>We are pilgrims on a journey
>Through the darkness of the night
>We are bound for other places
>Crossing to the other side
>
>I will worry 'bout tomorrow
>When tomorrow comes in sight
>Until then Lord I'm just a pilgrim
>Crossing to the other side
>
>Jesus will be there to meet me
>He will reach his hand in mine
>I will no more be a stranger
>When I reach the other side

(The flatboat has disappeared.)

Huck: What you going to do with your freedom, Jim?

Jim: Work hard, and never spend a single cent until I get enough to buy my wife.

Huck: I never knowed you had a wife, Jim.

Jim: She belongs to a farmer near St. Petersburg. Then we'll both work until we got enough money to buy our two children.

Huck: Take a heap of money for that.

Jim *(grimly):* If their master won't sell 'em, why then I'll hire an abolitionist to go steal 'em.

Huck *(to audience):* Then my conscience got to troubling me. This thing I was doing come home. Thinks I: Jim's going to get free. He's going to hire somebody to steal that farmer's property. And who's to blame for it? Me.

Jim: Pretty soon, I'll see the lights of Cairo. Then I'll be shouting for joy, and I'll say Huck done it! Jim's a free man, and it's all on account of Huck!

(A fog is gathering.)

Huck: Look—the stars is going out.

Jim: We're going into a fog. We'll miss Cairo!

Huck: I'll go forward and make some noise. We'll get run down, if we're not careful. *(Grabbing a tin pot, he goes forward and starts beating it with a spoon, shouting off into the fog.)* Yo there . . . Yo!

Jim: Look sharp, Huck! If we miss Cairo, it's all over for Jim. We'll just keep drifting down, deeper and deeper into the slave country.

Huck *(to audience):* My conscience was stirring me up, hotter than ever. I says to it—let up on me! I'll go ashore at first light and tell. *(Shouting.)* Yooo there . . . Yo!

Jim: Can you see anything?

*(A skiff appears, carrying **Two Men** with shotguns, poled by a **Slave**.)*

First Man: Who's that yonder?

Jim: You my friend, ain't you, Huck?

Huck: Hide, Jim—they got guns.

*(As the skiff pulls alongside, **Jim** hides under a blanket.)*

Second Man: What's your name, boy?

Huck: Uh . . . Sid Jackson.

First Man: Any men on this raft, boy?

Huck *(playing the innocent)*: One, sir.

Second Man: Five niggers run off tonight, up yonder above the bend. Is your man black or white?

Huck: He's . . . white.

First Man *(stepping onto the raft)*: I reckon we'll come on board and see for ourselves.

Huck: I wish you would, sir. Because it's my pa, and he's sick. And everybody goes away when I ask 'em to help me tow this raft ashore, and I can't do it myself.

First Man *(about to look under blanket)*: Well, that's infernal mean.

Second Man: Odd, too. Say, boy, what's the matter with your pa?

Huck: It's the smallp . . . well—it ain't nothing much.

First Man *(leaping back onto skiff)*: Boy, that's a lie.

Huck *(blubbering)*: Just don't leave us, please.

First Man: Keep away, boy. Confound it, your pa's got the smallpox, and you know it precious well. Why didn't you say so?

Huck: 'Cause I knew you'd go away, like the others.

First Man: Look, boy, here's a twenty-dollar gold piece. *(Tossing coin to* **Huck.***)* I feel mighty mean to leave you. But my kingdom, it won't do to fool with the smallpox.

Second Man *(tossing coin):* Here's twenty dollars from me, too. Good-bye, Sid! If you see any runaway niggers, get help and nab 'em, you can make some money by it.

Huck: Good-bye, sir. I won't let no runaway niggers by me if I can help it.

(The skiff is gone.)

(To audience, in the lantern-glow): I knowed very well I'd done wrong. Then I says to myself, hold on—suppose you done right and give Jim up. Would you feel better than what you do right now? No, says I—I'd feel worse. Well, then? What's the use in learning to do right, when it's troublesome to do right, and no trouble to do wrong, and the wages is just the same? *(Calling out.)* Jim! They're gone.

Jim *(emerging from the blanket):* Oh, Huck—that was the smartest dodge.

Huck: And we got twenty dollars apiece. That's deck passage on a steamboat to the Free States.

Jim: Jim ain't never going to forget this. You my only friend in the world, Huck—but you the best friend Jim's ever had.

(Thunder.)

Huck: I judge we should see Cairo by morning. But I'm bound to say I'll miss this ole raft.

Jim: Ain't no home like a raft after all, is there?

Huck: No—and nothing like floating down this river on a rainy night, mighty free and easy and comfortable.

(Rain falls. **Huck** *shares his blanket with* **Jim** *and they sing.)*

RIVER IN THE RAIN

Huck:
    River in the rain
    Sometimes at night you look like a long white
        train
    Winding your way away somewhere
    River I love you, don't you care

    If you're on the run
    Winding some place just trying to find the sun
    Whether the sunshine, whether the rain
    River I love you just the same

Jim:
    But sometimes in a time of trouble
    When you're out of hand and your muddy bubbles
    Roll across my floor

    Carryin' away the things I treasure
    Hell, there ain't no way to measure
    Why I love you more
    Than I did the day before

Huck & Jim:
    River in the rain
    Sometimes at night you look like a long white
        train
    Winding your way away somewhere
    River I love you, don't you care

Jim:
    But sometimes in a time of trouble
    When you're out of hand and your muddy bubbles
    Roll across my floor

Huck & Jim:
    Carryin' away the things I treasure
    Hell, there ain't no way to measure

Why I love you more
Than I did the day before
River in the rain
Sometimes at night you look like a long white
    train
Winding your way away from me

Huck:
    River I've never seen the sea

(At the conclusion of the song, the rain ends and they light cigars. They blow smoke into the air, and the sky is filled with clouds of stars.)

Just look at those stars. Think they was made? Or just happened?

Jim: I allow they was made.

Huck: I allow they just happened. It would a took too long to make so many.

Jim: But I allow the moon could a laid 'em.

Huck: Well, that looks kind of reasonable. I've seen a frog lay almost as many, so of course it can be done. *(Pointing.)* One just fell; what do you think that means?

Jim: I allow it got spoiled and was hove out of the nest.

Huck: These seegars is prime.

Jim: They sho' is.

Huck: It's lovely, living on a raft.

Scene 8

The stillness is shattered by a gunshot and the sound of barking dogs. **Two men** *appear on the bank, gasping, out of breath.*

King: There's a raft.

Duke: Ahoy there! Can you take us on board?

Huck: We ain't got room.

King: You've got to help us. We're in danger of our lives. Those dogs are following *us!*

Huck: What have you done?

King: Nothing, I tell you.

Duke: It's all a misunderstanding.

King: But we ain't got time to explain.

Huck: All right, come aboard.

(They pile on board. The **King** *is over fifty, gray-bearded; wears a slouch hat and a blue jean overcoat with brass buttons. The* **Duke** *is younger, and has a histrionic air. A* **Posse** *bursts out of the woods behind them, firing pistols, but* **Huck** *and* **Jim** *pole the raft vigorously, leaving them behind.)*

King: I reckon we gave them the slip.

Huck: You won't have to worry now—we'll be miles downstream by daylight. I'm wondering if you could tell us—how far is it to Cairo?

King: Cairo? Why, you're already in Kentucky, boy.

Huck: Then we floated right past Cairo in that fog.

Jim *(heavily):* So it's all up with Cairo.

King: That nigger belong to you?

Huck: 'Course he does.

King: You're mighty young to own him. He wouldn't be a runaway, would he?

Huck: For goodness sake, would a runaway nigger run *south?*

King: No, I allow he wouldn't.

Huck: Jim's my only belonging in this world. My pa was killed when this raft was run over by a steamboat. I've had considerable trouble with people not believing me and trying to take Jim away from me.

King: Do you reckon we could travel with you for a few days?

Huck: I guess that would be all right.

Duke: We'd be obliged to you.

Huck: You can sleep there on the deck, and when it gets light, we'll stop and have breakfast.

*(The **King** and the **Duke** huddle together, speaking softly.)*

Duke: Are we supposed to sleep on these rough planks? I could catch my death of pneumonia.

King: It beats that jail we just busted out of. What's your usual line of business?

Duke: Theater-actor—tragedy, you know. I also sell an article to take the tartar off the teeth. And it does take it off, too—and generally the enamel along with it. What about you?

King: Preaching's my speciality. And I done considerable in the doctoring way—laying on of hands for cancer, paralysis, and suchlike. Almost anything, so long as it isn't work. What say we go it together for a while?

Duke: I'm not indisposed.

(Day breaks as **Huck** *poles the raft ashore. The* **King** *and* **Duke** *get off,* **Jim** *prepares breakfast, and* **Huck** *speaks to the audience.)*

Huck: I didn't rightly know where we were going, now that we'd missed the Ohio. The raft wouldn't go upstream, of course. There was nothing to do now but keep on floating downriver; and as long as we were, no reason not to give 'em a lift. Anyway, I said to myself I'd sort of been feeling the need of a change again. The days had been sliding by so smooth they was almost dull. But the old raft was uncommon lively with them two along.

Duke *(addressing the dawn):*
Out, out, damned spot
For life 'tis but a tale told by an idiot
'Tis an unweeded garden that grows to seed
Throw physic to the dogs; I'll none of it.
(Louder.) Friends, Romans, Countrymen . . .

King: Is that chicken ready yet?

Huck: Almost.

Jim: I don't see why we got to give 'em any of this chicken.

Huck: We got to help 'em out, don't we? I'd expect people to do the same for me, if I was in trouble. *(Calling out.)* We can eat now.

King *(to* **Duke**): Ain't you going to join us?

Duke: Alas!

King: What are you alassin' about?

Duke: To think that I should have lived to be leading such a life, and be degraded down to such company.

King: Ain't the company good enough for you?

Duke: Yes, it's good as I deserve, for who fetched me so low when I was so high? Myself. One thing I know— there's a grave somewhere for me. Some day I'll lie down in it and forget all, and my poor broken heart will be at rest.

(They stare at him, dumbstruck by this astonishing performance.)

King: Well, what are you heaving your busted heart at us for? We ain't done nothing.

Duke: I'm not blaming you gentlemen; I brought myself down.

King: Brought yourself down from what?

Duke: You would not believe me! The world never believes—the secret of my birth. . . . But let it pass! 'Tis no matter.

King: All right, we'll let it pass.

Huck: No, I want to hear. What's the secret of your birth?

Duke: By rights, I am a Duke.

Huck: A Duke!

King *(drily):* No! You can't mean it.

Duke: Yes, my grandfather, eldest son of the Duke of Bridgewater, fled to this country to breathe the pure air of freedom before he died. He left two sons. The older robbed the younger of his title. I am his descendant—the rightful Duke of Bridgewater. And here am I, torn from my high estate, ragged and heartbroken and degraded to the companionship of felons on a raft! *(He breaks down.)*

Huck: How do you like that, Jim? We got a real Duke, right here on this raft.

Jim: S'wonderful, mighty wonderful.

Huck: Now, don't cry, you . . . your . . . what should we call you?

Duke *(stepping back onto raft):* Well . . . you might call me "Your Grace" or "My Lord" or "Your Lordship." But I wouldn't mind if you called me just plain Bridgewater.

Huck: Sure, we can do that.

Duke: And one of you ought to wait on me at dinner.

Gordon Connell

Bob Gunton, Evalyn Baron, Ron
Richardson (top), Daniel H. Jenkins,
Susan Browning and Rene Auberjonois

John Goodman and Daniel H. Jenkins

Bob Gunton, Rene Auberjonois and Daniel H. Jenkins

Ron Richardson and Daniel H. Jenkins

The BIG RIVER Company

Huck: We'll do any little thing for you that you want done, Your Grace.

Jim *(spooning chicken):* Will Your Lordship have some of this chicken? Here—this is the best portion.

Duke: Thank you. It's great comfort to hear you acknowledge me.

King *(who has been watching this in silence):* Look here . . . uh, Bilgewater. I'm nation sorry for you, but you ain't the only person who's been thrown down wrongfully from a high place, or had a secret of his birth. Can I trust you?

Duke *(taking his hand):* To the bitter death. Speak!

King: Bilgewater . . .

Duke: Bridgewater.

King: I am the late Dolphin.

Jim: The Dolphin, Huck! Just like you tole me!

King: Yes, friend, you are looking at the pore disappeared Dolphin, Louie the Seventeen, son of Louis Sixteen and Marie Antoinette.

Duke *(drily):* You? At your age? No! Why the Dolphin would be a youngster. You look six or seven hundred years old, at the very least.

King: Trouble has done it, Bilgewater—trouble brung these gray hairs, and premature balditude. Yes, gentlemen! You see before you, in blue jeans and misery, the wandering, exiled, trampled-on, sufferin' and rightful King of France.

Huck: King, we're mighty sorry for you!

Jim: But mighty proud we got you along, too.

Huck: How can we make *you* feel better?

King *(unhesitatingly):* Go down on one knee to speak to me, and always call me "Your Majesty."

Jim: Well, then, Your Majesty better have this portion. *(He takes the chicken leg off* **Duke's** *plate, transfers it to* **King's**.) And here's a portion for Your Lordship. *(The* **Duke** *looks at this smaller portion distastefully.)*

Huck *(to audience):* Of course, it didn't take me long to realize they weren't no real kings and dukes. But it tickled me to see the way they had ole Jim fooled.

King: What's matter, Bilgy? You don't have to be so stand-offish. Your family was a good deal thought of by my father. He allowed all the Dukes of Bilgewater to come to the palace considerable.

Duke: You know, I think you have the makings of an actor in you.

King: Me?

Duke: Has . . . Your Majesty ever trod the histrionic boards?

King *(flattered):* No. Hardly ever seen any playacting either—I, uh, was too small when Pa used to have 'em at the palace. Do you reckon you could learn me how?

Duke *(catching fire):* Easy. And it could be profitable. Very profitable!

King: Oh, we're going to make a great team, Bilgy. There's sheep to be shorn all up and down this river.

Duke: And you and me are just the people to do it.

(**Huck** *poles the raft into the current. The* **King** *and* **Duke** *step onto a floating log as it glides by.)*

WHEN THE SUN GOES DOWN IN THE SOUTH

When the sun goes down in the South
And the moon comes up in the East
Step right up and see the wonder of the ages
It's a guaranteed visual feast

King:
When the darkness falls on the town
And the North Star's startin' to rise

King & Duke:
Well, you can't imagine the menagerie air
Created by a couple of guys

Duke:
Well, anybody wonderin' what they're going to see
Gonna have to ante up a dollar for the ticket

King:
Anybody wonderin' what's goin' on

King & Duke:
Is gonna find out when they chase us through the
thicket

When the darkness falls on the town
And the North Star's startin' to rise
Well, you can't imagine the menagerie air
Created by a couple of guys

(They step ashore.)

Duke: I'm used to playing Romeo, so you can be Juliet.

King: But Juliet's a young gal, ain't she? My peeled head and my white whiskers is goin' to look uncommon odd on her, maybe.

Duke: These country jakes won't ever think of that. Besides, you know, you'll be in costume, and that makes all the difference in the world. Now: Juliet's in a balcony, enjoying the moonlight before she goes to bed. Repeat after me: "Romeo, Romeo, wherefore art thou?"

King *(bellowing):* "Romeo . . . Romeo, wherefore art thou?"

Duke: No, no, no. Juliet's a mere child of a girl. She doesn't bray like a jackass! *(Capering downstage.)*

King & Duke:
> When the sun goes down in the South
> And the hayseeds stand in line
> Step right up and see the duo bodily
> Do the do wah ditty on the clothesline
>
> When the darkness falls on the town
> And the North Star's startin' to rise
> Oh, you can't imagine the menagerie air
> Created by a couple of guys

King: This ain't no bad thing, Bilgy. We got transportation, grub, and the boy's a flathead who could be useful.

Duke: So he could.

King: And if nothing else—we can always sell the nigger. *(Calling to* **Huck.***)* Come along, my boy!

*(***Huck*** leaps up to join them.)*

Jim: Huck!

King: Come along!

Duke, King & Huck:
>When the sun goes down in the South
>And the moon comes up in the East
>Step right up and see the wonder of the ages
>It's a guaranteed visual feast
>
>When the darkness falls on the town
>And the North Star's startin' to rise
>Oh, you can't imagine the menagerie air
>Created by a couple of guys

Duke:
>Anybody wonderin' what they're going to see
>Gonna have to ante up a dollar for the ticket

Huck:
>Anybody wonderin' what's goin' on

Duke, King & Huck:
>They're gonna find out when they're chasin' us
>   through the thicket

(Stepping back onto the raft.)

>When the sun goes down in the South
>And the North Star's startin' to rise
>Oh, you can't imagine the menagerie air
>Created by a couple of guys
>You can't imagine the menagerie air
>Created by a couple of guys

(Huck *poles the raft so that it turns downstage.)*

King, Duke & Huck:	Jim:
When the sun goes	
Down in the South	Look out for me
And the moon comes	Oh muddy water
Up in the East	
	Your mysteries
Step right up and see	
The wonder of the ages	Are deep and wide
It's a guaranteed visual feast	

When the darkness
Falls on the town
And the North Star's
Startin' to rise
You can't imagine
The menagerie air
Created by a couple of guys

You can't imagine
The menagerie air
Created by a couple of guys

I got a need

For goin' some place

And I got a need to climb
Upon your back and ride

I got a need
I got a need to climb
Upon your back and ride

ACT TWO

Scene 1

*The onstage musicians appear and play the overture to Act Two. At its conclusion, the raft, carrying **Huck**, **Jim**, the **King** and **Duke**, glides on stage.*

Huck: We drifted on down pretty much into the state of Tennessee, and I was having a gay old time studying those rascals. When they weren't rehearsing Shakespeare, the King showed me how to do card tricks; and the Duke lectured on the science of phrenology. They had as many schemes as a possum does ticks. And I was learning a lot from their monkeyshines.

(King *and* **Duke** *are rehearsing a duel with wooden swords.)*

Duke: Eh la! Eh la! Eh la! Un, deux, trois, quatre, cinq, six. Un, deux, trois. No, no, no, no, no . . .

King *(bellowing):* "Romeo, Romeo, wherefore art thou!"

*(The **King** attacks the **Duke** with the flat of his sword and knocks him down.)*

Duke: Enough! This is hopeless.

King: I'll get her yet, Bilgy. I'm agoing to knock the spots off any acting you ever saw.

Duke: No. What we shall perform is a different type of drama altogether.

King: You mean we won't be doing Shakespeare?

Duke: These yokels aren't up to your Juliet. They want comedy—low comedy—maybe something rather worse than low comedy. And I have just the role for you.

King: Do you?

Duke: You secure the African. You, boy, come with me—and see that you follow every move I make.

Scene 2

Duke *and* **Huck** *cross to Bricktown, Arkansas, where three* **Loafers** *sit in the sun.*

Huck: So the Duke and me went into Bricktown, Arkansas, to look for some paying customers. Why they called it Bricktown, I don't know—there wasn't a brick in the whole place. The one street was nothing but mud. And the only people in sight was an onrey-looking bunch of loafers.

Hank: Give me a chaw of tobacco, Lafe.

Lafe: I just give my last one to Andy.

Andy: What are we going to do today, Lafe?

Lafe: Too hot to do anything, Andy.

Andy: Maybe there'll be a dogfight later on.

Lafe: I hope so. Ain't nothing to wake me up and feel happy all over like a good dogfight.

Andy: What's say we pour turpentine on a dog and set fire to him? That's better than a dogfight.

(**Huck** *and the* **Duke** *approach them,* **Huck** *with hand-bills.*)

Duke: Gentlemen, gentlemen, give a listen! All willing and able should step right up and follow me to the Bricktown wharf, to purchase their tickets for the show of the century!

Hank: What's he so excited about?

Lafe: It's another one of them medicine shows.

Duke: Tonight! On the stage of the shipwrecked show-boat *Sir Walter Scott,* the sublime poetry of William Shakespeare, and a freak of nature, brought to you from the jungles of Borneo at great expense, the Royal None-such!

Andy: Royal Nonesuch? What's a Royal Nonesuch?

Duke: How shall I describe it? It is neither a son of Adam, nor a daughter of Eve, but partakes of the characteristics of both.

THE ROYAL NONESUCH

She's got one big breast
In the middle of her chest
And an eye in the middle of her nose
So says I, if you look her in the eye
You're better off looking up her nose

Whoever you are, wherever you've been
You've come this far
Well come on in
See the Nonesuch

Huck:
    Nonesuch

Lafe:
    Nonesuch

Andy:
    Nonesuch

(More townspeople appear, played by onstage **Musicians***.)*

Duke:
    I get up early, I stay up late
    I've seen it before
    But I still can't wait
    To see the Nonesuch

Musician no. 1:
    Nonesuch

Musicians no. 2 and no. 3:
    Nonesuch

Loafers:
    Nonesuch

Duke & Huck:
    She's got one big breast
    In the middle of her chest
    And an eye in the middle of her nose
    So says I, if you look her in the eye
    You're better off looking up her nose

Hank: How much?

Duke: Only fifty cents, the one-half part of a dollar. Servants, ten cents. Because the Nonesuch will be exhibited in a state of nature, no ladies will be permitted. But the education of no man or boy is complete until he has witnessed this shocking spectacle!

Andy: No ladies permitted?

Hank: Sounds plumb disgusting.

Lafe: Well, what are we waiting for?

(**Tarts** *appear in the windows of a brothel.*)

Duke:
>Believe you me, it's the best of the best
>I know what I'm saying
>I've seen the rest
>The Nonesuch

Tart no. 1:
>Nonesuch?

Tart no. 2:
>Nonesuch

Tart no. 3:
>Nonesuch

Duke:
>It'll strike you blind
>With a heave and a sigh
>But come up close enough to risk one eye
>For the Nonesuch

Tart no. 1:
>Nonesuch

Tarts:
>Nonesuch

Men:
>Nonesuch

Duke & Huck:
>She's got hound dog ears that hang down to here
>And lips like the bud of a rose
>So says I, if you look her in the eye
>You're better off looking up her nose

Tarts:
> She's got hound dog ears that hang down to here
> And lips like the bud of a rose
> So says I, if you look her in the eye
> You're better off looking up her nose

(Slaves *appear on wharf, loading goods.*)

Duke: Only fifty cents, the one-half part of a dollar. Servants, ten cents.

> I've been to Natchez and to New Orleans
> But this beats anything I've ever seen
> The Nonesuch

Slave no. 1:
> Nonesuch?

Slaves no. 2 and no. 3:
> Nonesuch

All:
> Nonesuch

Duke:
> I've seen your money,
> I can see your face
> Now come on in and take your place
> For the Nonesuch

All:
> Nonesuch, Nonesuch, Nonesuch

Duke & Huck:
> Well, it ain't no woman and it ain't no man
> And it don't wear very many clothes
> So says I, if you look her in the eye
> You're better off looking up her nose

(*The curtained stage of the showboat descends into view, and the people of Bricktown crowd in.*)

Servants, Tarts, and Loafers *(overlapping):*
> Well, it ain't no woman and it ain't no man *(etc.)*
>
> She's got hound dog ears that hang down to here
>
> She's got one big breast in the middle of her chest
> And an eye in the middle of her nose
> So says I, if you look her in the eye
> Then you're

All:
> Better off looking up her
> Better off looking up her
> Better off looking up her
> One big breast in the middle of her chest
> And an eye in the middle of her nose

*(The **Duke,** who has disappeared behind the curtain, reappears, holding a skull, and the **Crowd** falls silent.)*

Duke:
To be, or not to be; that is the bare bodkin
That makes calamity of so long life;
For who would fardels bear, till Birnam Wood do come
> to Dunsinane
But that the fear of something after death
Murders the innocent sleep.
And makes us rather sling the arrows of outrageous
> fortune
Than fly to others that we know not of.
There's the respect must give us pause:
Wake Duncan with thy knocking! I would thou couldst;
For who would bear the whips and scorns of time,
And the quietus which his pangs might take,
In the dead waste and middle of the night, when
> churchyards
Yawn in customary suits of solemn black,
But that the undiscovered country from whose bourne
> no traveler returns,
Breathes forth contagion on the world,

And, like the poor cat in the adage,
Is sicklied o'er with care,
Tis a consummation devoutly to be wished.
But soft you, the fair Ophelia, Nymph
Ope not thy ponderous and marble jaws,
But get thee to a nunnery—go!

(The Duke bows.)

Crowd *(impatiently):* Nonesuch! Nonesuch! Nonesuch!
(etc.)

Duke: Thank you! Thank you! That was Hamlet's immortal soliloquy. And now for the second part of our show. Gentlemen! Presenting the most shocking spectacle ever performed! The incredible . . . *(The Duke signals for a fanfare.)* The unbelievable . . . The Royal Nonesuch!

(Fiddle music. The King appears, wearing an outlandish hermaphroditic costume that includes a wig, breasts, hooves, and woollen leggings. He clog-dances around the stage uncomfortably before showing the audience his woolly behind and disappearing to roars of laughter.)

This great tragedy will be performed only two nights more, on account of pressing London engagements. The seats are already sold for it in Drury Lane.

Hank: That's all there is to it?

Duke: If we have succeeded in pleasing and instructing you, we hope you'll mention the show to your friends. *(Bows and starts to go.)*

Man in Crowd: Tar and feather them tragedians!

(The Crowd roars with anger and pelts the stage with cabbages and tomatoes. Lafe leaps onto the stage and fires his pistol into the air.)

Lafe: Hold on! We been took—mighty badly took. But we don't want to be the laughingstock of the whole town. No, what we want to do is talk this show up and sell the rest of the town—then we'll all be in the same boat. Now ain't that sensible?

Hank: Lafe's right.

Lafe: Now let's go home, and invite everybody else to see the tragedy tomorrow night.

(Still grumbling, the **Crowd** *leaves.)*

Duke: Greenhorns! Flatheads! How much did we make?

Huck: One hundred and thirty-five dollars.

Duke: No women or children—I knew that would fetch them!

Huck: Look here, Your Grace, we got away with it to-night. But what about tomorrow? I got an idea they might want to make things hot for us.

Duke: Tomorrow? Why, they come to the theatre . . . we take their money as usual . . . they take their seats . . . and then . . .

Huck: Yeah?

Duke: We'll shin for the river, like the dickens was after us.

(The **King** *reappears, still in Nonesuch costume.)*

King: Never again!

Duke *(laughing at him):* You were magnificent! You hauled in a wagonload of money. And tomorrow—

King: There ain't going to be any tomorrow! There's got to be a way of making money that don't involve turning me into a public spectacle. We're leaving tonight!

(**King** *and* **Duke** *exit, and the showboat stage flies out.*)

Huck: The King and the Duke went off to celebrate, and I went back to the raft, thinkin' how great them two was, how they'd made fools of the whole town and a pot of money besides.

Scene 3

Huck *crosses to the raft.* **Jim,** *chained to the deck, sits with a blanket wrapped around him. His face is smeared with blue clay, and there is a sign hung around his neck which reads: "SICK ARAB—BUT HARMLESS WHEN NOT OUT OF HIS HEAD."*

Huck *(to audience):* The raft was pulled up in this little cove. By now, them two were keeping Jim chained up all the time. And when I seen the getup they made him wear so people wouldn't think he was a runaway, I just had to laugh! *(Laughs.)*

Jim: Huck?

Huck: I decided to play a joke on him. *(Disguising his voice.)* Look yonder!

Jim: Who's there?

Huck: Ain't that a runaway? I believe it is. Let's get him, boys!

Jim *(leaps up, holding a stick):* Don't come any closer, whoever you are! I'll knock your brains out! *(When* **Huck** *dances out, laughing.)* Oh, Lord God, it's you!

Huck: Oh, Jim, that was so comical! Of course it's me! You simpleton! But I guess you'd believe just about anything, wouldn't you? *(Dissolves into laughter again.)*

Jim: Don't you do me that way, Huck Finn!

Huck: Blamed if you aren't the horriblest-looking outrage I ever did see, Jim. You look like a man that's been drowned nine days!

Jim: I was so thankful to see you I could have got down on my knees and kissed your foot. And all you were thinking about was making a fool of Jim. Well, go on—get your face out of my sight.

Huck: Now, Jim, don't be talking trash—

Jim *(angrily):* You the one who's trash! Trash is people who puts dirt on the heads of their friends, and makes 'em ashamed.

Huck: Oh, all right, just sit there! *(Crosses away. Pause. To audience:)* It was almost fifteen minutes before I could work myself up to go and humble myself before a nigger —but I done it. *(Defiantly.)* And I weren't ever sorry for it either! *(To* **Jim:**) I'm sorry, Jim.

Jim: You just come here, Huck. *(They embrace.)* We's all right now. But, Huck—I reckon these ain't no real kings after all.

Huck: No, Jim. I reckon they're low-down frauds and humbugs. But we got to go along with them for your sake.

Jim: Can't we just get shut of them, so things can be like they was before? *(When* **Huck** *does not reply.)* You'll think of something, Huck. You the only white person ever kept his word to Jim.

(As **Huck** *helps* **Jim** *clean the clay from his face, they sing.)*

WORLDS APART

Jim:

I see the same stars through my window
You see through yours
But we're worlds apart
Worlds apart

I see the same skies through brown eyes
That you see through blue
But we're worlds apart
Worlds apart

Just like the earth, just like the sun
Two worlds together are better than one
I see the sunrise in your eyes
That you see in mine
But we're worlds apart
Worlds apart

Huck:

I see the same stars through my window
That you see through yours
But we're worlds apart
Worlds apart

And you see the same skies through brown eyes
That I see through blue

Both:

But we're worlds apart
Worlds apart

Just like the earth, just like the sun
Two worlds together are better than one
I see the friendship in your eyes
That you see in mine
But we're worlds apart

Worlds apart
Together, but worlds apart

Jim:

And a mockingbird sings
In the ol' yonder tree
Twaddle-ee ah dee dee dah dee dee dee

S'hard. S'mighty hard. Poor little Elizabeth . . . poor little Johnny.

Huck: Are those your children, Jim?

Jim: Those are my children, and I spec I'll never see 'em no more! S'funny, but I can hardly sleep now, Huck, for thinking about them. Last night, I hear somebody slam a door way over on the other shore. It remind me of when my Elizabeth was four years old, and just got over a rough spell of scarlet fever. One day I says to her, "Shut the door." But she just stands there, kind of smiling at me. So I says again, might loud, "Do you hear me?—Shut the door." She done me the same way. I was a-boiling, so I says, "I lay I *make* you mind!" And I fetch her a slap upside the head that sent her flying *(He closes his eyes, rocks back and forth; presently.)* I go in the other room, and when I come back ten minutes later, she still standing there, tears streaming down her face. Before I could hit her again, long come the wind and slam the door to, blam! And my Lord, *the child never move.* My breath hopped right out of me. Oh, Huck! I burst out cryin' and grab her. Lord God Almighty forgive Jim, I says, 'cause he ain't never going to forgive himself as long as he live! That fever left her deaf and dumb, Huck. Plumb deaf and dumb. And I'd been treating her so.

Huck *(to audience):* It don't sound natural, but Jim cared for his people just as much as white folks do for their'n.

*(The **King** and **Duke** enter, wearing new clothes and hats.)*

Duke: Good morrow to you, my boy.

Huck: Duke? Why we got to keep Jim chained up all the time? There's nobody to see.

Duke: No, no, no, my boy. Chains are the correct thing, at all times. We must preserve the unities, as they say on the boards.

Huck: King, I reckon Jim and me will be going our own way now.

King: I reckon you won't. Why, the Duke and me was just going to make you a partner: we think you got the possibilities.

Huck: I don't want any part of your schemes—

King: That nigger ain't yours. You're a nigger-stealer, my boy: it's clear. And if you think anyone would take the word of a scoundrel boy over two fine gentlemen like ourselves, you got another think coming; so let's not hear any more high-toned talk. Now—what's that there town?

Duke: Hillsboro.

King: Let's drop over and see if we can't get some sort of project going. Now that we got these store-bought duds, we can pass for rich folks, and we won't have to try the Nonesuch no more. *(To* **Huck.***)* Adolphus—that's you.

Huck: Yes, Your Majesty?

King: Come along. You're my valet now.

Scene 4

Huck, King, *and* **Duke** *cross to the Hillsboro ferry slip, where a* **Young Fool** *waits, sitting on his trunks and singing to himself.*

YOUNG FOOL ARKANSAS

Arkansas, Arkansas
I just love ole Arkansas
Love my ma, love my pa,
But I just love ole Arkansas

Well, I ain't never traveled much
But someday when the money's such
I'd like to see the world and all
And take a run through Arkansas

Huck *(to audience):* So we walked to the town of Hillsboro, where we met a young fellow waiting for a steamboat who told 'em everything they needed to know.

Young Fool:
I'd like to get my picture took
And put it in my memory book
And someday hang it on my wall
To say that I'd seen Arkansas

King, Duke, Young Fool:
Arkansas, Arkansas
I just love ole Arkansas
Love my ma, love my pa,
But I just love ole Arkansas

Young Fool: Could you be the Reverend Harvey Wilkes?

King: . . . I could be.

Young Fool: Well, I'm sorry to say you ain't come on time, Reverend. Your brother Peter died last night.

King: Oh no . . .

Young Fool: And to think you come all the way from Sheffield, England; and you ain't seen your brother since you were six years old. It's so sad.

King (*affecting a ludicrous English accent*): Terrible sad, but we all got to go one way or the other, don't we?

Young Fool: Yes, sir, that's what my mother used to say. But you'd better get over to your brother's house right now. He left a letter with your niece, Mary Jane, saying how he wanted all his property divided up.

King: Did he now? (*Indicating* **Duke**.) You're a clever young man, ain't you? But I'll bet you can't tell me who this is.

Young Fool: Certainly. It's your poor afflicted brother William, who's deaf and dumb.

(**Duke** *nods, making mute sounds.*)

Good day, Reverend. I'm off to visit my uncle in Rio Janeero.

King: Well, good day to you, my boy; and God's blessing on you. (*As they cross away.*) Bilgewater, did you get all that?

Duke: I did.

King: Then get ready to give the performance of your life. We're going to take these flatheads for all they're worth. Being brothers to a rich dead man is the line for you and me, Bilgy. Come along, Adolphus.

YOUNG FOOL:
>Grandpa he was always good
>I'd play horsey on his foot
>He'd tell me when I'd get tall
>We'd both go see Arkansas

>Arkansas, Arkansas
>I just love ole Arkansas
>Love my ma, love my pa,
>But I just love ole Arkansas
>I just love ole Arkansas

(As **King, Duke,** *and* **Huck** *exit, the interior of the* **Wilkes** *home appears. There is a sofa down center, and a doorway at the top of the flight of steps. The Wilkes sisters—***Mary Jane, Susan,** *and* **Joanna**—*enter, dressed in black, followed by a* **Servant, Alice,** *and her daughter,* **Betsy.** **Mourners** *also enter, carrying a coffin, which they place on trestles down right. They sing, overlapping the* **Young Fool.**)

HOW BLEST WE ARE

Mourners:	Young Fool:
How blest we are	
As children of a God	Arkansas, Arkansas
So good and true	I just love ole Arkansas
To understand	Love my ma, love my pa, but
His moving hand	I just love ole Arkansas
And love for me and you *(Exits.)*	

How blest we are
As children of a God
Whose love is real
Enough to touch each one of us
Is part of Him I feel

I honor Thee, I honor Thee
To whom my love is vowed
How blessed be
Forever we are bound to Him as now.

Betsy:
> How blest we are
> As children of a God
> So good and true
> To understand His moving hand
> And love for me and you
>
> How blest we are
> As children of a God
> Whose love is real
> Enough to touch each one of us
> Is part of Him I feel
>
> I honor Thee, I honor Thee
> To whom my love is vowed
> How blessed be
> Forever we are bound to Him as now

(As the hymn ends, **Huck,** *the* **King,** *and the* **Duke** *appear in the doorway.)*

King: Is this where Mr. Peter Wilkes lives?

Servant: This is where he did live . . . he's over there, on ice. He went to glory, yesterday afternoon.

(The **King** *crosses dramatically to the open coffin, throws himself down, kisses the lips of the corpse. All come to their feet.)*

King: Alas! My poor brother, gone—and we never got to see him! Oh, it's too, too hard!

Mary Jane: You must be my Uncle Harvey.

King: I'm Harvey. This is William. And you, my dear child, must be Mary Jane.

Mary Jane: I am. And these are my sisters, Susan and Joanna.

Huck *(to audience, as* **King** *gives* **Mary Jane** *a long, lascivious kiss):* One was stone-faced, and one had a harelip. But Miss Mary Jane was real pretty.

Mary Jane *(producing a letter and a bag of gold dollars):* Here's a letter my father left behind.

King *(reading):* Why, let's see . . . it gives the house and three thousand in gold to you . . . and six thousand in gold to William and me.

Mary Jane *(handing him the bag):* And here it is.

King: Let us pray! My poor brother that lays yonder has done generously by those of us that's left behind in this vale of sorrows. And we know he'd a done more generously by his daughters if he hadn't been afraid of wounding William and me. What sort of uncles would we be that'd rob such poor lambs as these, who he loved so? *(Over the frantic protestations of the* **Duke.***)* Here, Miss Mary Jane—take the six thousand.

(Murmurs of approval from the **Mourners. Mary Jane** *is almost overcome.)*

Mary Jane: You dear good souls! How could you?

Counselor Robinson: My God!

Mary Jane: Why, Counselor!

Counselor Robinson: These aren't your uncles. They are nothing but the thinnest kind of imposter!

King *(trying to embrace him):* Is this my brother's dear friend and adviser—

Counselor Robinson: Keep your hands off me, you ignorant tramp! Oh yes, you talk like an Englishman—don't you? Why, it's the worst imitation I've ever heard!

Mary Jane: But he knew our names. And if they were imposters, why should they refuse my father's legacy?

Counselor Robinson *(taking her hand):* Mary Jane Wilkes. I was your father's friend, and I'm your friend; and I warn you as a friend, and an honest one, to turn these pitiful scoundrels out of your house and have nothing more to do with them. Will you?

Mary Jane: Here is my answer. *(Giving the bag of money back to the King.)* Keep the money! All of it. Invest it for me any way you choose. We open our house and heart to you; and I place myself and my affairs completely in your hands!

Huck: It was enough to make a body ashamed of the human race.

(The Mourners clear the stage.)

The King sent everyone home and tole 'em to come back tomorrow, when he was a-going to preach his brother's funeral sermon. Miss Mary Jane fed them two frauds and tole them they could sleep right there in the house. She and her sisters was wonderful people, and I says to myself it just ain't right to let that old reptile rob her of her money. So that night, after the late sounds had quit and the early ones hadn't begun, I slipped upstairs and took the gold. I judged I'd better hide it somewhere . . .

(As Huck crosses downstage with the bags of gold, the Sisters appear, holding candles.)

Then I heard somebody coming!

(**Huck** *hides the gold in the coffin and conceals himself.*
Mary Jane *sits by the coffin;* **Susan** *and* **Joanna,** *up left
and right.*)

YOU OUGHTA BE HERE WITH ME

Mary Jane:
>   If you think it's lonesome
>   Where you are tonight
>   Then you oughta be here with me
>   If you think there's heartaches where you are to-
>   night
>   Then you oughta be here with me

Mary Jane & Joanna:
>   Because with you I'm whole
>   Without you I'm cold

Mary Jane:
>   If teardrops are fallin' where you are tonight
>   Then you oughta be here with me

Mary Jane, Joanna, & Susan:
>   Loneliness calling where you are tonight
>   Then you oughta be here with me

>   Because with you I'm whole
>   Without you I'm cold

Mary Jane:
>   So if you think about me
>   Where you are tonight
>   Then you oughta be here with me.

(They blow candles out.)

Huck: I almost out and told 'em. But I was so ashamed of
where I'd hid the money, the words just dried up in my
throat.

Scene 5

Daylight floods the stage. The organ plays and the Sisters *are joined by the* Mourners, *the* King, *and the* Duke. *The* King *clears his throat and addresses the* Mourners.

King: Dear friends . . . before my brother is laid in the ground, I want to say how glad we are to see everybody here at his funeral orgy. We wanted to make this a public funeral orgy—

(The Duke *makes frantic sounds.)*

Poor William, afflicted as he is, his heart's always right. He wants me to make everybody welcome. But he needn't worry, that's just what I'm at. Everybody should be here, for my brother respected everybody. Therefore, it's fittin' that his orgies should be public.

(The Duke *had been scribbling furiously; he hands a note to the* King, *who reads it, then goes on.)*

I say orgies, not because it's the common term, because it ain't—obsequies being the common term—but because orgies is the right term. Obsequies ain't used in England no more—it's gone out. We say orgies now, in England. Orgies is better, because it's exact. It's a word made up out'n the Greek *orgo,* outside, open, abroad; and the Hebrew *jeesum,* to plant, cover up, hence, inter. (**Mourners** *gasp and shift uncomfortably.)* Anyhow, let's not linger here any longer, but bid goodbye to him that lies yonder, cold but joyful!

(Organ plays and the Mourners *carry out the coffin.)*

HOW BLEST WE ARE (REPRISE)

Mourners:
    I honor Thee, I honor Thee
    To whom my love is vowed
    How blessed be
    Forever we
    Are bound to Him as now

Huck *(to audience):* The music sounded mighty good, after all that soul-butter and hogwash.

(He watches them carry the coffin to the cemetery and lower it through a trap in the stage floor.)

We walked to the cemetery, and I watched them screw the lid on that coffin, and lower it into the ground. In trying to better this, I've worsened it a hundred times, and I wished to goodness I'd just let it alone, dad-fetch the whole business!

(The **Mourners** *have exited and the* **Sisters** *have returned to the house.* **Alice** *and* **Betsy** *appear.)*

Alice: Miss Mary Jane!

Mary Jane: Alice!

Alice: They sold us! Your uncle done it! He sold my girl to Memphis . . . and he sold me downriver to New Orleans! I'll never see my little girl again as long as I live!

Mary Jane *(to* **King**)*:* What is this?

King: Miss Mary Jane, my congregation will be worried about me and my brother if we don't get back, so we got to settle the estate right now and leave. So I'm auctioning off your house and selling your slaves, and I want you and your sisters to come to England.

Mary Jane: England!

King: You can make a fresh start there, and your relatives'll be honored to take care of you.

Mary Jane *(in shock):* But you can't separate Alice and her daughter!

King: You placed your affairs completely in my hands, Miss Mary Jane. What's done is done.

(He exits, leading off **Betsy.** **Alice** *cries out and exits in the other direction, followed by* **Susan** *and* **Joanna.***)*

Huck *(to audience):* It busted my heart to see them women crying for grief. So I decided I'd chip in and change the general tune.

(He crosses to **Mary Jane,** *who sits alone on the sofa crying softly.)*

Could I have a word with you, Miss Mary Jane?

Mary Jane: Yes.

Huck: I've been watching you, and . . .

Mary Jane: Please go on.

Huck: You got more grit than any girl I ever seen. In my opinion, you're just full of grit, Miss Mary Jane. Does that sound like flattery?

Mary Jane: No. Thank you, Adolphus. I've been watching you too, and I think you're a fine young man. *(She puts her hand on his.)*

Huck *(to audience):* She lay her silky hand on mine, and I thought I would just about die. *(To* **Mary Jane:***)* I just wish you wouldn't grieve so.

Mary Jane: How can I help it, knowing Alice and her daughter will never see each other again.

Huck *(impulsively):* But they will—inside of two weeks. I know it.

Mary Jane *(gripping him):* Say it again, say it again, say it again!

Huck: Just let me think a minute. *(To audience:)* Here's a case where I'm blessed if it doesn't look like the truth is actually safer than a lie. I never seen nothing like it. So I says to myself—I'll chance it this time, though it does seem like sitting on a powder keg and touching it off just to see where you'll go. *(Turning back to* **Mary Jane.***)* There's something you got to know.

Mary Jane: Yes?

Huck: Don't you holler; just sit there and take it like a man.

Mary Jane: I'll do the best I can.

Huck: Those uncles of yours ain't uncles at all—they're frauds.

Mary Jane *(leaping up):* I knew it! I knew it! Come on—don't waste a minute. Let's go tell the sheriff.

Huck: Hold on! If you blow on them, there'll be another person named Jim, who'll be in big trouble.

Mary Jane: I'll show them trouble! I'll have them tarred and feathered and thrown into the river!

Huck: Look: the sale of your slaves won't count when it comes out they're imposters. Leave the house long enough for me and Jim to get away, then go to the sheriff.

Mary Jane: All right . . . I will.

Huck: There's one thing—that bag of money.

Mary Jane: Well, they've got it; and it makes me feel pretty silly to think how.

Huck: No, they ain't got it. I hid it.

Mary Jane: Where?

Huck: In . . . I'd rather not tell you. But I'll leave a note.

Mary Jane: All right. I'll do everything you told me. Must you leave? If you were to stay, I should be your truest friend.

Huck: No, I got to go.

Mary Jane: Good-bye. I shan't ever forget you. But I'll think of you many a time—and I'll pray for you, too! *(She kisses him on the lips; then exits.)*

Huck *(to audience):* Pray for me! I reckon if she'd knowed me, she'd a-taken on a job that was nearer her size. But I'll bet she done it. She had the grit to pray for Judas, if she took the notion; and when it come to beauty and goodness, she lay over them all. I ain't never seen her since she went out of that door. No, I ain't never seen her since. But I reckon I thought about her many and many a million times.

(Stage darkens. **Mary Jane** *appears down left,* **Jim** *down right.)*

LEAVIN'S NOT THE ONLY WAY TO GO

Huck:
>Did the morning come too early
>Was the night not long enough
>Does a tear of hesitation
>Fall on everything you touch
>Well, it might just be a lesson
>For the hasty heart to know
>Maybe leavin's not the only way to go

Mary Jane:
>Maybe lay and let your feelings
>Grow accustomed to the dark
>And by morning's light, you just might solve
>The problems of the heart
>And it all might be a lesson
>For the hasty heart to know
>Maybe leavin's not the only way to go

Jim & Mary Jane:
>People reach new understandings all the time
>They take a second look
>Maybe change their minds

Jim, Huck & Mary Jane:
>People reach new understandings everyday
>Tell me not to reach

Huck:
>And I'll go away

Jim, Huck & Mary Jane:
>Did the morning come too early
>Was the night not long enough

Huck:
>Does a tear of hesitation
>Fall on everything you touch

Jim, Huck & Mary Jane:
>Well, it might just be a lesson
>For the hasty heart to know

Huck:

> Maybe leavin's not the only way to go

> And a heart without a home
> Is such a lonesome row to hoe
> Maybe leavin's not the only way to go

(**Mary Jane** *and* **Jim** *disappear.*)

Huck: Now it was time for me to light out for the raft—

Scene 6

As **Huck** *starts for the door, the* **King** *and the* **Duke** *enter on the run, followed by* **Movers** *who start carrying out the furniture.*

King: Boy! Were you in our room last night?

Huck: No, but this morning I seen the slaves tiptoe in and out.

Duke: Great guns, this is a go!

Huck: I thought they was doing up your room, and found Your Majesty asleep.

King: We got to swallow it and say nothing. We can still make a pile with the auction.

Duke: Our luck's run out.

King: Oh, shut up! *(To* **Huck:**) Stay there, you little nit. *(To* **Movers:**) Not you, get moving!

Duke: Maybe we should slide out of here while we still can.

King: And leave this property? Why, there's eight or nine thousand dollars worth of goods lying around here, just suffering to be sold. Here's what you do, Bilgy. Go to the raft and sell that boy's nigger. Take what you can get, so long as it's enough for two steamboat tickets out of here. The moment the auction's over, we'll vanish!

Duke: I'll do it.

King: And see you come back. (**Duke** *exits. The* **King** *crosses back to* **Huck,** *who has been edging out.)* Where are you going?

Huck: Just out for some air, Your Majesty.

King *(sliding a concealed knife out of his cane):* I'm not completely satisfied you're telling the truth . . .

(A crowd of hooded men has appeared at the door. Among them is **Sheriff Bell,** *and a white-haired gentleman with an authentic English accent, who is the real* **Harvey Wilkes.)**

Are you gentlemen here for the auction?

Sheriff: I'm Sheriff Bell.

King *(turning away):* . . . It don't start for another hour.

Harvey Wilkes *(coming downstage):* We're not here for the auction, my good man; we're here to ask you some questions.

King: Well, who do you think you are?

Harvey Wilkes: The real Harvey Wilkes.

King: Mf! It gives me a stomachache in my very heart to think there could be such frauds in the world.

Sheriff: We got two heirs contendin' here, and I don't know which is authentic—you pays your money and you takes your choice. But the first thing I want to know is, where's the nine thousand dollars in gold Miss Mary Jane give you?

King: Alas, the slaves stole it.

Sheriff: Uh huh. I'm pretty satisfied you ain't real, but for all I know, you're both imposters.

Harvey Wilkes: I've thought of something. Is there anyone here who helped lay out my brother?

Man in Crowd: Me and Ab Turner done it.

Harvey Wilkes: Then—*(Turning to* **King**.) perhaps this gentleman can tell us what was tattooed on his breast.

King: Uh . . . mf! That's a tough question, ain't it. Yes, sir, I can tell you. It's just a small thin blue arrow—that's what it is!

Harvey Wilkes: Nonsense! What you saw were the initials P . . . B . . . W in very faint blue ink. Isn't that correct?

Man in Crowd: No. I never saw no tattoo at all.

Crowd *(roaring):* They're all frauds! Let's drown 'em! Let's duck 'em! Let's ride 'em out of town on a rail!

Sheriff *(shouting):* Gentlemen, if you please! There's only one way to settle this, let's go dig up the corpse and look!

(Lightning and thunder. The **Mob** *drags* **Huck,** *the* **King,** *and* **Harvey Wilkes** *to the cemetery, growing in number and chanting as they go.)*

Mob: Tar and feather 'em, tar and feather 'em, tar and feather 'em, tar and feather 'em, oil 'em and boil 'em, tar and feather 'em. Ride 'em out of town on a rail.

(Reaching the cemetery, the **Mob** *gathers around the open grave.)*

Huck *(to audience):* I was scared now, I can tell you. This was the most awful trouble, and the most dangersome, I'd ever been in. Everything was going so different from what I had allowed for.

Robinson: Here's the coffin!

(Thunder. **Sheriff Bell** *drops into the grave with a crowbar to force the coffin lid. Everyone leans forward.)*

Huck: I kept hoping Miss Mary Jane would show up—but it didn't look like she was going to.

Sheriff: By the living jingo, here's the bag of gold on his breast!

(He holds up the bag. The **King** *reaches for it greedily. Everyone is frozen by a blinding flash of lightning. There is a long, rolling boom of thunder, and the stage goes black.)*

Scene 7

Huck *flees through the darkness to the river where the raft is moored.*

Huck *(to audience):* When everyone tried to bust in for a look, I lit out for the road! I had it all to myself, and how I did clip along! And somehow in the dark, and the rain, I found my way back to the raft. *(Shouting.)* Jim! It's me, Huck! We're all right now! *(Sees the raft is empty.)* But Jim was gone. Figuring he busted the chain, I sat down and waited for him. *(Lights lantern.)* I waited for hours.

Duke *(offstage):* Aaahhh.

Huck: Jim?

*(The **Duke** appears, coated with tar and feathers, the hot tar smoking on the damp night air.)*

Duke: Help me.

Huck: Duke? Is that you?

Duke: I've got to have some water. I'm dying of thirst.

Huck: Where's Jim?

Duke: I sold him.

Huck: You sold him?

Duke: I got forty dollars from a farmer.

Huck: After all this long journey, and after all we done for you, you made him a slave again all his life, and among strangers, for forty dirty dollars!

Duke *(staggering toward the river):* I got steamboat tickets, first class, for our escape. The mob met me on the way back. I told the King we should have slid. If only he hadn't been so greedy. *(Stoops to drink from the river and sees his reflection.)* Look at me! I look like a nigger myself.

Huck: You look pretty funny! It's what you deserve! *(Kicks him viciously.)* Who'd you sell him to?

Duke *(sobbing):* Silas Phelps. He lives two miles down the road.

Huck *(suddenly sorry):* Can you stand up?

Duke *(struggling painfully to his feet):* Oooh, it's so hot in here. I can't get any air! You've got to help me! I'll never get out of here. Never. I'll die in here!

(He staggers off and disappears.)

Huck *(to audience):* Much as he'd done to me, I couldn't feel any hardness against him. Human beings can be so cruel to each other. It hit me all of a sudden that here was the hand of God, letting me know I'd been watched all along from above . . . and people who helped a nigger like I'd done were the ones who went to the everlasting fire. I decided to pray and see if I could stop being the kind of boy I was. But you can't pray a lie, I found that out. I'll write a letter—*then* see if I can pray. *(Crosses to raft; gets paper and pencil and scribbles.)*

"Miss Watson. Your runaway nigger Jim is down here two miles south of Hillsboro and Mr. Phelps will give him up for the reward if you send. Huck Finn." *(Standing.)* I felt light as a feather, washed clean of sin for the first time in my whole life! But then I got to thinking about our trip down the river and I seen Jim before me all the time, and we a-floating along, talking, singing and laughing. And him saying I was his only friend in the world. . . . *(Suddenly he tears up the letter and flings the pieces away.)* All right, then, I'll go to hell! I'll take up wickedness again, which is in my line, being brought up to it. And for a starter, I'll steal Jim out of slavery again. And if I can think of something worse, I'll do that too: because as long as I'm in, and in for good, I might as well go whole hog!

(As **Huck** *sings, the sun rises and the river is again revealed.* **Phelps Slaves** *appear, pulling a wagon full of cotton.)*

WAITIN' FOR THE LIGHT TO SHINE
(REPRISE)

Huck:
> Well, I have lived an undirected life
> A cloudy way I know, the only way I knew
> And so the things I've done, in fact each and every one
> Are the way that I was taught to run

Huck & Women Slaves:
> I am waitin' for the light to shine
> I am waitin' for the light to shine
> I have lived in the darkness for so long
> I'm waitin' for the light to shine

Huck & Men Slaves:
> Far beyond horizons I have seen, beyond the things
> I've been, beyond the dreams I've dreamed
> Are the things I've done, in fact
> Each and every one
> Are the way that I was taught to run

Huck & Slaves:
> I am waitin' for the light to shine
> I am waitin' for the light to shine
> I have lived in the darkness for so long
> I'm waitin' (waitin') I am waitin'
> Everybody here is waitin' (waitin')
> Lord I'm (waitin') are you (waitin')
> Truly (waitin') yes I'm (waitin')
> I am waitin' for the light to shine

> I am waitin' for the light to shine
> I am waitin' for the light to shine
> I have lived in the Darkness for so long

I am waitin' for the light
I am waitin' for the light
I am waitin' for the light to shine (the light to
    shine)

Scene 8

Huck *travels along a country road.*

Huck: At first light, I set off looking for the Phelps place, down a country road, still and Sunday-like. It was all hot and sunshiny, and there was nobody in sight until I come to a big double log cabin.

(Sounds of barking dogs. **Sally** **Phelps** *emerges from the cabin, wearing an apron.)*

Sally: Tige! Spot! You hush up that racket now, you hear! *(Seeing* **Huck.***)* It's *you*—ain't it?

Huck: Yes'm.

Sally *(hugging him):* You don't look as much like your mother as I reckoned you would; but land sakes, I don't care for that, I'm so glad to see you. Come in and let me have a *good* look at you.

Huck *(following her—to audience):* I went along, trusting to Providence to put the right words in my mouth. I'd noticed it always did, if I just let it alone.

Sally *(seating him at table and cutting him a piece of apple pie):* We've been expecting you all week. What kept you? Boat run aground?

Huck: No, ma'am. Blowed a cylinder head.

Sally: Don't say ma'am, say Aunt Sally. Your Uncle Silas went to town to fetch you; he'll be back any minute. He got started late 'cause he bought a runaway slave yesterday. A stranger sold his chance in him for forty dollars.

Huck *(to audience):* So I knowed I'd found the Phelps place.

Sally: Silas had to fix him a place in the shed, down by the ash-heap. I expect he'll be able to sell him for a good piece of money. But you ain't told me a word about Sister, yet. *(Sitting across from him.)* Now you tell me *everything*— how the folks are; what they're doing; what they told you to tell me; and every last thing you can think of.

Huck *(to audience):* I seed I was up a tree.

Sally *(looking past him):* Here comes Silas! Hide under the table and we'll play a joke on him.

(Huck *does as she says.* **Silas Phelps** *has entered, followed by his* **Slaves,** *a rifle on his shoulder.* **Slaves** *sit upstage, the women sewing a blanket and* **Silas** *crosses wearily to the house.)*

Silas *(deadpan):* He ain't come.

Sally: Oh my goodness gracious, where in the world could he be?

Silas: I don't know what to make of it. I'm at my wits' end, and I don't mind acknowledging it.

Sally: Look yonder, ain't that him coming up the road?

Silas: Where?

(As he looks, Sally *signals* Huck, *who comes out from under the table.* Silas *turns, sees him, points his rifle at him.)*

Who are you?

Sally: Who do you reckon?

Silas: I ain't no idea.

Sally: It's *Tom Sawyer!*

Huck *(to audience):* I almost slumped through the floor.

Silas *(pumping his hand):* Ain't seen you since you was a baby. You've growed.

Sally: This is a joyful moment.

Huck *(to audience, as they sit at table again):* If they were joyful, it weren't nothing to what I was. I was so glad to find out who I was, it was like being born again.

Silas: I been looking for you every day this week.

Sally: His boat blowed a cylinder head.

Silas: Anybody hurt?

Huck: No, sir. Killed a nigger.

Silas: Well, it's lucky because sometimes people do get hurt. Two years ago last Christmas, I was coming up from New Orleans on the old *Lally Rock.* She blowed a cylinder head and crippled a man. I think he died thereafter. He was a Baptist.

Huck *(to audience):* Then I got to thinking: S'pose the real Tom Sawyer steps in here any minute? I'd better go up the road and waylay him. So I told the Phelps I was going back for my baggage . . .

(He slips across the stage. Silas, *who had been talking through this, continues as lights fade on his area.)*

Silas: . . . Yes, I recollect now he did die. Mortification had set in and they had to amputate him. Yes, it was mortification—he turned blue and died in the hope of a glorious resurrection. They say he was a sight to look at.

(Huck, *crossing the stage, encounters* Tom Sawyer, *carrying a small suitcase.)*

Huck *(to audience):* Sure enough, before long I seen him coming. *(To* Tom:) Hold on!

Tom *(unable to believe his eyes):* What do you want to come back and haunt me for? I never done you no harm!

Huck: I ain't come back—I never been gone.

Tom: Honest Injun, you ain't a ghost?

Huck: Honest Injun.

Tom: But look here: weren't you ever murdered at all?

Huck: Not at all. I played it on 'em. Come here and feel if you don't believe me.

Tom *(does):* What have you been doing with yourself?

Huck: Having a grand, mysterious adventure that I ain't got time to tell you about right now.

Tom: I'm visiting my aunt, Sally Phelps.

Huck: I know. I'm there right now—playing *you.* Now listen. Your Uncle Silas has got Jim locked in his shed.

Tom: Ole Miss Watson's Jim?

Huck: He's been traveling along with me. Here's the important thing, Tom. I'm going to steal Jim out of slavery!

Tom: But you don't need—

Huck: I know what you'll say. It's a dirty, low-down business, but what if it is? I'm low-down too, and I'm going to steal him, and you won't let on, will you?

Tom *(gleefully):* I'll *help* you steal him.

Huck: You're joking.

Tom: I ain't joking.

Huck: I'm bound to say, you just fell considerable in my estimation. Tom Sawyer a dirty abolitionist? I can't believe it.

Tom: Well, I'm a-going to do it. Didn't I say I was going to?

Huck: Yes.

Tom: *Well,* then.

Huck: All right, here's my plan: I fetch my raft.

Tom *(nodding):* Raft.

Huck: Then, first dark night, I steal the key to the shed from your uncle's britches.

Tom *(nodding):* Britches.

Huck: We release Jim, then shove off downriver. Won't that work?

Tom: Work? Certainly, but it's too simple. What's the good of a plan that ain't no more trouble than that? It's mild as goose milk. Let me think.

Huck *(to audience):* So he thought.

Tom: We'll dig him out.

Huck: Dig?

Tom: With spoons. It should take about a week. As things stand, it's just too simple. That's what makes it so rotten difficult to come up with a difficult plan. I bet there ain't even a watchdog to give sleeping mixture to. I bet there ain't even a moat. If we get time, the night of the escape we might dig one. How's that sound?

Huck *(to audience):* I seen Tom's plan was worth fifteen of mine for style. It would make Jim just as free, and might get us both killed besides. *(To* **Tom:**) I'm satisfied.

Tom: Bully! Let's go look at that shed.

(They cross to the shed, where **Jim** *sits on a small stool.)*

Huck *(to audience):* It was just a little shed with a padlock on the door and a board nailed across the window. *(To* **Tom:**) We can bust this board right out, Tom.

Tom: I should hope we can find a way that's a little more complicated than that, Huck Finn.

Jim *(peering out window):* Why, Huck! And good land! Ain't that Tom?

Huck: We're here to set you free, Jim.

Jim: I could a got out this window hole long time ago, only how am I going to travel with a ten-foot chain on my leg?

Tom: Lemme think.

Huck *(to audience):* So he thought.

Tom: No, it wouldn't do. There ain't enough necessity for it.

Huck: For what?

Tom: Chop Jim's leg off.

Jim: There ain't no necessity for it!

Tom: Well, some of the best authorities has done it. He's got to have a rope ladder—we'll send it in a pie—and he can write notes, using rust and tears for ink, like "Here a captive heart busted." That's what the Iron Mask done.

Huck: Look, Tom! I'm all for the adventure of digging him out, but maybe we could simplify the plan. Your uncle's going to be selling Jim pretty soon, so we ain't got forever.

Tom: Well, that's so.

Huck: You hide in the woods and come back tonight at moonrise. I'll bring the spoons. So long, Jim.

Jim: See you tonight, Huck.

(Huck *exits.)*

Tom: Oh, Jim—you got any spiders in there?

Jim: Bless you, Tom, I don't want none. I'd just as soon have a rattlesnake.

Tom *(thinking):* It's a good idea. Where could you keep it?

Jim: Keep what?

Tom: A rattlesnake.

Jim: Tom—

Tom: You could tame him, Jim, by singing songs to him, so he'd love you, and sleep with you, and let you put his head in your mouth for a favor.

Jim: I lay he'd wait a powerful long time before I'd ask him.

Tom: Here you are, loaded down with gaudier chances than any prisoner ever had to make a name for yourself, and you won't even try. Don't you see the sense in it?

Jim *(angrily):* No, I don't see the sense in it! But then, you're white folks.

Tom: If only we had more time, we could keep it up all the rest of our lives, and leave Jim to our children to get out. We could spread it out over eighty years, if I had my way . . .

(He exits. **Jim** *sings, joined by* **Phelps Slaves** *upstage.)*

FREE AT LAST

Jim:
    I wish by golly
    I could spread my wings and fly

And let my grounded soul be free
For just a little while

To be like eagles when
They ride upon the wind
And taste the sweetest taste of freedom
For my soul

Then I'd be free at last
Free at last
Great God Almighty
I'd be free at last

Jim & Phelps Slaves:
To let my feelings lie
Where harm can not come by
And hurt this always hurtin' heart
That needs to rest awhile

I wish by golly
I could spread my wings and fly
And taste that sweetest taste of freedom
For my soul

Then I'd be free at last
   (free at last)
Free at last
   (free at last)
Great God Almighty
I'd be free at last
   (free at last)
I'd be free at last
   (free at last)
I'd be free at last
   (free at last)
Great God Almighty
I'd be free at last
   (free at last)
I'd be free at last
   (free at last)
Oh, Lord, I'd be free at last
   (free at last)

Great God Almighty
I'd be free at last

(**Jim** *and* **Slaves** *stand.*)

I'd be free at last
(free at last)
I'd be free at last
(free, free, free at last)
Great God Almighty
(I'd be free, I'd be free)
At last

Scene 9

Darkness falls. **Phelps Slaves** *disappear.* **Huck** *and* **Tom** *dig a hole under the foundation of the shed with spoons.*

Huck *(to audience):* That night, we busted Jim out of captivity.

Tom: It'd only take a few more days.

Huck: We ain't got a few more days . . . here's a cold chisel, Jim. Knock that chain off your foot. *(Hands hammer and chisel to* **Jim** *through window.)*

Jim *(breaking chain):* That done it!

(He scrambles through the hole and into **Huck's** *arms. As he does, a* **Figure** *appears upstage carrying a rifle.)*

Silas: Who's there?

Huck *(whispering):* Get back! What's Uncle Silas doing here?

Tom: He's come to stop us from stealing Jim.

Huck: How'd he find out?

Tom: Because I wrote him an anonymous letter from an unknown friend, saying there was a gang of cutthroats here from the Indian Territory, and stealing Jim was their hellish design.

Huck: What'd you do that for!

Tom: After all this hard work and trouble? Why, this escape would go perfectly flat without somebody to prevent it.

Jim: I think that's the way I would have liked it.

Tom: I'll distract him, then you escape. Meet you at the raft!

(**Tom** *leaps up and runs across the stage, giving a loud yell.* **Silas** *fires.* **Huck** *and* **Jim** *flee to the raft.*)

Huck *(to audience):* Jim and I ran for the river. The dogs was after us, making powwow enough for a million, but when we reached the raft the sound of 'em got dim and died out, and I knew we was safe. *(To* **Jim:**) Did he make it?

(**Tom** *appears.*)

Tom!

Tom: Now, Jim, you're a free man again.

Jim: It was a mighty good job. It was planned beautiful, it was done beautiful, and nobody else could think of a plan as mixed-up and splendid as that. I'm mighty glad to be free.

Huck: And I'm mighty glad that job's over.

Tom: And I'm gladdest of all, 'cause I got a bullet in my leg. *(Falls into their arms.)*

Jim: He's losing blood.

Tom: Boys, we done elegant. Now you got to get on that river before they catch you, Jim. You too, Huck.

Jim *(tying a rag around* **Tom**'s *wound):* You bet we don't.

Tom: Both of you shove off; I'll be all right here.

Jim: I don't budge a step out of this place without a doctor, not if it's forty year.

Huck: I'll get to town and get one.

Tom: All right, but first you got to blindfold him and swear him to silence, and give him a purse of gold . . . *(Faints.)*

Jim: Tom!

Huck: Hide in the woods when you hear us coming, Jim. Hide until the doctor's gone! (**Huck** *runs off.)*

Jim: Hurry, Huck. I can't stop the bleeding!

(**Huck** *crosses the stage to the doctor's office. There are* **four Patients** *waiting outside in chairs. The* **Doctor,** *who sits behind a desk, is played by* **Mark Twain.***)*

Huck: When I got to town that morning, I shoved right past the sick people waiting outside the doctor's office. *(To* **Doctor:**) Me and my brother was camping out on Spanish Island and he got shot and you got to come right away!

Doctor: Just simmer down, boy, and tell me. Who's your folks?

Huck: The Phelps, down yonder.

Doctor: Oh. *(Raising.)* How'd you say he got shot?

Huck: He had a dream. And it shot him.

Doctor: Singular dream.

Huck: I mean, he must have kicked the gun in his dreams, and it went off and shot him in the leg. And you've got to come right now and not tell anybody, because we're supposed to be home tonight and we want to surprise our folks!

(Silas Phelps has entered.)

Doctor: Mr. Phelps, this may be one of the people you're looking for. Do you know him?

Silas: That's my nephew Tom, who disappeared last night.

Doctor: He says his brother's been shot in the leg and is lying sick over on Spanish Island.

Silas: He ain't got a brother.

Doctor: You see, boy, Mr. Phelps come here because some people stole his slave last night. He thinks he wounded one, and they might be looking for a doctor. Would you know anything about that?

Huck: I ain't talking.

Silas *(Grabbing **Huck**)*: Who are you, then? Be you one of the gang who stole my nigger!

Doctor: He don't look too dangerous to me, Silas. *(Picking up his bag.)* I'm going to Spanish Island and see if I can get to the bottom of this.

Silas: You oughtn't go alone. Wait, and I'll send a couple of my men along with you.

Doctor: Send 'em after me. If somebody's hurt, I don't intend to wait around. *(He goes.)*

Silas *(Grimly, manhandling* **Huck**): You better loosen your jaw, boy. You got a heap of talkin' to do. (**Phelps** *drags* **Huck** *out.)*

(The **Doctor** *crosses to the island where the raft is tied up.* **Jim** *is holding* **Tom's** *head in his lap. When he hears the* **Doctor** *approach, he hides.)*

Doctor: Is there anybody here?

Tom *(delirious):* Man the raft, boys . . . don't stop now . . . let's go booming down the river!

Doctor *(examining him):* Hold still, boy. You're one sick little cuss. *(Opens bag.)*

Tom: What are you going to do?

Doctor: Well, for a start I'm going to take my scalpel and cut that bullet out of your leg. You're a brave boy, aren't you? Bite this here stick and hold still as you can.

Tom: If you chalk my raft, I'll kill you!

Doctor: Chalk your raft?

Tom: So you can find it later.

Doctor: Boy, I'm a doctor.

Tom *(struggling):* I'll kill you, I say. Man the raft, boys! Man the raft!

Doctor: Oh, Jesus, Mary and Joseph. I got to have some help somehow.

(He takes a bottle out of his bag. Instantly, **Jim** *is out of the bushes and at his side.)*

Jim: I'll help.

Doctor: You'd be the runaway slave.

Jim: You be the doctor, that's the only thing that's important here. What you got the bottle for? We need a doctor, not a drunk.

Doctor: I was only going to pour whiskey on his wound to clean it.

Jim: See that's the only place you pour it.

*(***Doctor*** pours whiskey on* **Tom's** *leg.* **Jim** *holds* **Tom.** **Doctor** *picks up scalpel.* **Jim** *looks him in eye.)*

(Evenly.) See you do your job . . . do it good.

Doctor: Hold him still.

*(***Tom*** cries out as the area fades to black.)*

Scene 10

Interior of the **Phelps** *home.* **Huck** *sits in a chair, his face closed like a fist.* **Silas Phelps** *regards him grimly.* **Sally Phelps** *is also there.*

Silas: My nephew disappeared. My slave stolen. It's unbelievable. That shirt I found out in the shed, covered with secret African writing done in blood. What does that mean? And what about that rope ladder cooked in a pie. What was it for? Why, there must have been forty or fifty of you, but lo and behold, you still got away with that slave right under my nose! Where's the rest of your gang? Boy, if you don't unbutton your lip, you're in for a power of misery.

Huck: I ain't talking.

Silas *(taking off belt):* Maybe what you want is a taste of this. *(Brings belt smashing down on back of chair.* **Huck** *jumps involuntarily.)*

Sally *(bursting out):* No, Silas! *(To* **Huck:***)* We don't want to hurt you. We just want to know what you done with my sister's boy, Tom. Did you kidnap him? You see, Mr. Phelps and I never had any children of our own. I promise no harm will come to you, if you'll just tell me what you've done with Tom.

Huck: Tom and me done it. We both knowed Jim up in Missouri—that's the slave. We done it, and it took a power of work. Tom wrote the anonymous letter. And the dogs didn't follow us because they knew me and weren't interested. We got to the river and our raft, and Jim was a free man, and wasn't it bully, as Tom says.

Sally: But where's Tom?

Huck: On Spanish Island. *(To* **Silas:***)* You put a bullet in his leg.

Silas: I shot my own nephew . . .

(Upstage, two **Field Hands** *bring in* **Tom** *on a litter. He is covered with a blanket, his eyes closed. Following are the* **Doctor** *and a third* **Field Hand** *holding a shotgun on* **Jim***, whose hands are chained together.)*

Sally: Oh, he's dead, he's dead. I know he's dead! *(Throws herself down by the litter.)*

Huck: Tom? You dead?

Tom *(eyes still closed):* No.

Doctor: He'll be all right. I got out the bullet.

First Field Hand: You caused a lot of trouble, nigger. We ought to make an example of you.

Third Field Hand: We ought to hang you.

Doctor: Don't you be rough with him! *(Filling his pipe.)* He saved this boy's life. And he throwed away his freedom to help me doctor him. I tell you, Silas, a man like that is worth a thousand dollars, in my opinion—and kind treatment, too.

Silas: Well, then, we'll not chain him this time. Just lock him up and see he gets a pot of greens now and then.

Tom: You won't lock him up!

Sally: You lay still.

Tom: You ain't got no right to lock him up. Turn him loose! He ain't no slave, he's as free as any creature that walks this earth!

Sally: Good land, that child's out of his head.

Tom: No I ain't out of my head! *(Struggling up.)* Ole Miss Watson, who Jim belonged to, died two months ago. She was so ashamed she was ever going to sell him downriver she set him free in her will! It's true, Jim!

Sally: Then what on earth did you want to set him free for, seeing as how he was already free?

Tom: If that ain't just like a female. I wanted the adventure of it, and I'd have waded knee-deep in blood to get it!

Jim: Tom . . .

Silas: Let him go.

(The **Field Hand** *releases* **Jim.***)*

Jim: I 'preciate what you done. But you should a told me.

Tom: Oh, but you don't know what I had in mind, Jim. After we got you out safe, we were going to get on that raft and have adventures plumb down to the mouth of the river. Then I was going to tell you you were free, and take you home on a steamboat, in style. And write word ahead and get out all the slaves around for torchlight procession and a brass band. Then you'd be a hero, and so would we. *(To* **Aunt Sally.***)* I guess I'm in a heap of trouble.

Sally: You're alive, that's all that matters—though I could most skin you, for all the worry you've caused me.

(The two **Field Hands** *carry* **Tom,** *in the litter, offstage,* **Sally** *and the* **Doctor** *following.* **Silas Phelps** *looks at* **Jim.***)*

Silas: Strike the chains off that nigger.

(The **Field Hand** *restraining* **Jim** *unlocks the chains, which fall to the floor with a crash.)*

RIVER IN THE RAIN (REPRISE)

Huck *(coming downstage):*
    River in the rain

Sometimes at night you look like a long white
    train
Winding your way away somewhere
River I love you, don't you care

If you're on the run
Winding someplace just trying to find the sun

Jim *(joining him):*
    Whether the sunshine, whether the rain

Huck & Jim:
    River I love you just the same

Huck: Then Jim and me went down to the river, and for a
long time we sat there, listening to the sound of it going
on, heading out toward the sea. *(To* **Jim:**) I told you we had
luck.

Jim: So you did.

Huck *(lightly):* Here's a notion. Let's slide out of here,
soon as Tom's leg's better. We'll buy some horses and go
for some howling adventures amongst the Indians, over in
the Territory. How's that sound?

Jim: I got to head north, Huck.

Huck: What for?

Jim: Why, to do what I said. Go to the Free States and
make enough money to buy my wife and children.

Huck: Oh.

Jim: I'll be real glad to see those children again.

Huck: 'Course you will, Jim. I clean forgot about 'em.

Jim: Why not come with me as far as St. Petersburg.

Huck: No, I don't want to go back there, somehow. *(Pauses.)* Well, it's Pap. If I went back, Pap would just show up again, sure as you're born.

Jim: You never going to see your pap again, Huck.

Huck: Why do you say that?

Jim: I just know.

Huck: Spill it.

Jim: That dead man we saw floating in the river that night, early on? The one I wouldn't let you look at? That was him. *(When **Huck** says nothing, **Jim** rises.)* Whatever road I go walkin' down, you'll be walkin' alongside of me. The old true Huck.

(Jim goes.)

Huck *(to audience):* Then he left me alone, and I thought about all we'd done. It had been like the fortune he predicted for me, long ago. Considerable trouble and considerable joy. *(He rises.)* So that's how things fell out. Tom's almost well now. Jim's gone north. There's nothing more to show you and I'm rotten glad, because if I'd a knowed what trouble it was to enact this history, I never would a tackled it; and I ain't a-going to no more. I'm lighting out for the western territories ahead of the rest; because Aunt Sally, she's going to adopt me and civilize me and I can't stand it. I been there before.

(Huck walks up the steps and toward the river as the stage fades to black.)